CATHOLIC
PERSPECTIVES

Divorce

by
Mary Durkin
and
James Hitchcock

THE THOMAS MORE PRESS
Chicago, Illinois

ISBN: 0-88347-101-9

CATHOLIC PERSPECTIVES

Divorce

PART ONE

by
Mary Durkin

INTRODUCTION

DIVORCE is one of those disturbing topics that we would rather not think about unless we are required to by personal involvement or professional demands. I was somewhat hesitant when asked to reflect on the Catholic position on divorce since I had given little attention to the subject. During my student days at a Protestant divinity school I had not encountered any serious discussion of the issue. One professor, a divorced and remarried man, made a passing reference to the fact that some recent biblical scholarship calls into question the position that Jesus absolutely forbade divorce and remarriage, but no one bothered to follow up on that point. After completing my studies many issues commanded my attention. Divorce was one issue, but it was far down on my list of concerns.

Undoubtedly, my own ambivalent feelings were part of the reason divorce never found its way to the top of my priorities. Having grown up in a religious environment which viewed the Catholic Church as the one institution interested in saving family life from the destructive influence of divorce, I was not sure that this position should change. Admittedly, my response to the issue of divorce was largely emotional. Strong memories of divorce being forbidden not only by divine law as expressed by Christ, but also by the natural law, mingled with concern for what happened to children when their parents divorced. These were accompanied by a fear of the effect a change in the church position might have on young people when they encountered problems in marriage. Wouldn't they just quit when the going got rough? Didn't every married person have times when he or she might walk out if it weren't that we believed in the indissolubility of marriage? Where would young people find role models of happy life-long commitment if people were free to break up a marriage at will? But at the same time, some of my close friends were experiencing the pain of divorce and were in need of understanding and support from their religious community.

The more conversations I had with other Catholics the more I discovered that I was not alone in my ambivalence. The increase in annulments granted by the Church, as well as the increased numbers of divorced Catholics who have withdrawn from active participation in the Church, has made Catholics conscious of the fact that there is erosion within the Church on the issue of divorce; but, for the most part, the rationale for and the implications of this erosion are not understood. The request to examine the Church teaching on divorce and identify those elements which should be considered in developing a new perspective on this subject forced me to consider divorce as a concern of pastoral theology and to overcome the prejudices which previously had led me to avoid indepth reflection on the topic.

The focus which a new perspective on divorce should take became apparent when I realized that, inevitably, when the subject of the Catholic Church and divorce is touched upon in a group of adult Catholics, someone recounts the tale of her "Aunt Millie." Due to the Church teaching, Aunt Millie had to lead a lonely life for thirty years, and "those boys really could have used a father." Sometimes Aunt Millie's husband was a heavy drinker, or else an enemployed bum who left her after the birth of the fifth child, or maybe a psychopath who beat her twice a week, or a playboy who eventually left her for a younger woman. But in every case Aunt Millie had a tough life. The complaint being voiced today springs from a realization that there has been some change in the Church position, and a resentment that Aunt Millie did not have the benefit of the understanding being offered today.

Catholic Perspectives: Divorce

The concern for the Aunt Millies of the world gives us the primary focus which any attempt at a new perspective on divorce should take. We do not need another Catholic perspective on divorce as an abstract concept. We need a Catholic perspective on people who divorce. This is not a situation ethics approach to divorce. Rather it is an approach that realizes that it is people who divorce, people who suffer from divorce and people who need the help and support that the Church could offer through reconciliation and healing. In the past, concern for the institution of marriage often led the Church to neglect its responsibility of Christian concern for people. A new Catholic perspective must deal with what is going on in the lives of people who divorce and with how the Church position might best help them restructure their lives and deal with the problems that confront them.

A Catholic perspective on divorce is closely linked to one's understanding of the reason for a Church. The growing lack of agreement of Catholics with the Church's stand on issues of human sexuality[1] springs, in part, from conflicting impressions given by various statements and pronouncements of the hierarchy. In a period of transition from the older, hierarchial model of Church to the post-Vatican II People of God model, both the hierarchy and the general membership of the church are experiencing confusion on the need for and the role of authority. Church reform on divorce in a People of God model requires a new approach to pastoral theology which responds to the pluralistic nature of the Church.[2] It also necessitates that a new perspective on divorce be developed out of the shared perspectives of various Church communities as these are critiqued by the central beliefs of the Christian story.

The Church is a human institution which has the right to establish standards which help it achieve its reason for existence. If its teachings on divorce develop out of its understanding of both its mission *and* the situation to which it speaks, then it has the right and obligation to establish the means for gaining acceptance of this teaching among its members. If the experience of members has been considered in the development of the perspective, they will be more inclined to be responsive to the teaching.

To develop such a perspective here it is necessary to have some understanding of the situation of divorced individuals in today's world, to analyze the roots of the Church teaching on the indissolubility of marriage, to evaluate the current practices of the marriage tribunals, and, from the insights gained in this process, to develop a new perspective on the subject of the Church and people who divorce.

This examination of a Catholic perspective on divorce will limit itself to the experience of divorce in advanced technological societies. Obviously this experience is not identical with that of all parts of the world; but it is *one* experience which must be considered and responded to by the Christian community. Though the response might differ from place to place, all responses must find their foundations in an interpretation which is attempting to be faithful to the central vision of Christianity.

Although these reflections are on the topic of divorce, it is well to bear in mind that there is an intrinsic relationship between marriage and divorce. Any new perspective on divorce must grow out of a deepened understanding of the sacramentality of marriage. Without this understanding the Church will be forced either to maintain its strict legal sanctions against divorced individuals or to discover new interpretations of the legal requirements for marriage which will allow broken marriages to be annulled. In neither instance will the Church be meeting the needs of contemporary society for a vital theology of marriage and a sympathetic understanding of the problems of divorced individuals.

I

THE SHATTERING OF A DREAM

Everyone loves a wedding. There is something contagious about the spirit that surrounds preparations for marriage, and the ceremony seems to highlight the hope that is displayed by two people commiting themselves to a life-long love. In spite of the statistics which indicate a high percentage of marital breakups, two people are taking the risk that the love they feel for each other is strong enough to help them through the various crises of life.

Perhaps it is the incurable romantic in us that makes us continue to hope that marriages will work, or maybe it is the need we all have to hope that some people in our midst will be able to stick to a commitment. To promise oneself to another for the remainder of one's life, in the present culture, is either the most extreme folly based on complete naivete or a sign that even in the midst of the complexities of technological society, two people are able to work at a love relationship. At weddings we tend to believe the latter.

For this reason we are uncomfortable with divorce, and are content to have a superficial understanding of the reasons for and the complexity of divorce and of the needs of persons who are involved in it. Just as we rejoice at a wedding, seeing it as a new birth of something good and beautiful, we are dismayed at divorce since it seems to be the death of a dream. Just as we are uncomfortable with the mourner and the mourning process at the time of death, we do not want to deal with the issue of the death of hope and dreams and trust which are mirrored in the ending of a marriage.

No matter how broadminded a person is, the obvious fact that a promise is now unfulfilled is cause for concern. Not only the couple, but also the children, the extended family and friends have an investment in a marriage, and all feel dismay at the time of divorce. Even the ardent supporters of the human potential movement, who would hold that the imperative to actualize one's potential requires the right to divorce if a marriage interferes with that imperative, will admit that divorce is a traumatic experience not to be undertaken lightly.

So, contrary to the popular assumption that those who divorce take the easy way out, divorce is a trying situation. Those who advocate friendly divorce, or who see the natural right to divorce as important as the natural right to marry, look forward to the day when couples who choose to end a marriage will do so with decorum and will exercise wisdom in the way they deal with each other, their children, and anyone else concerned. Though it should be hoped that divorcing individuals would act in a mature manner, it is naive to think that divorce can occur without causing a great deal of grief.

In some instances both partners realize that the marriage was a mistake, find other interests, and mutually arrive at the decision that they will both be better off apart. Even then, they have to deal with the reactions of family and friends, most of whom do not condone this kind of decision. In most instances, however, there is one partner who has a stronger need to end the marriage, and he or she must handle the guilt that accompanies this inability to be faithful to a promise. The other partner also has to manage his or her sense of failure at not being able to meet the needs of a spouse, even when the spouse has failed to meet his or her needs.

The reasons for divorce are undoubtedly as complex as the reasons people choose to marry. Though the acknowledged cause might be, "He's having an affair and wants to be free," or, "Her drinking has made her impossible to live with," or, "He hit me once too often," these, and similar manifestations of trouble in a relationship, usually are not the real reason a marriage fails. The basis of marital discord can usually be traced back to the expectations the partners had regarding marriage and their own and their spouse's role in marriage. When either one or both partners are unwilling or unable to negotiate a reasonable attempt to meet these expectations, the marriage can become so intolerable that they are no longer able to live together in some semblance of peace and harmony.

The increase in divorce in technological societies can be traced to greater expectations of fulfillment in marriage, longer lives (previously many intolerable marriages ended due to the death of one partner), greater opportunities for women to support themselves if they find a marriage intolerable, increased acceptance of divorce, and lessening of the complications involved in legal divorce. The rise in the number of divorces, however, does not necessarily mean that there is an equal increase in the number of unhappy marriages. Many marriages in previous generations, when legal strictures against divorce were severe, were emotionally dead even though the couple continued to live together. When divorce was legally impossible, marriages "ended" through desertion, extra-marital affairs, cessation of sexual relations, and involvement with children or career. Even today some marriages that do not end in divorce cease to be love relationships.

What happens to the person involved in a divorce and how they cope with the feelings which occur at the various stages of divorce will have a considerable bearing on their future. If children are involved it also will influence how they manage the disruption in their lives. If a religious community is to respond to the needs of its members who are in this situation, then the community must be aware of the experience of divorce from the perspective of the effects it has on the lives of the individuals most affected. The issue of remarriage after divorce would depend on our perception of the necessity of marriage to the human development of an individual. We must examine whether remarriage after divorce is forbidden as punishment for past sins or as an attempt to avoid a repeat of the trauma caused by divorce.

We should begin by acknowledging that divorce is a traumatic situation which entails loss, grief and guilt. It creates a stress in the lives of those who experience it comparable to the stress suffered at the time of the death of a spouse or discovery of a terminal illness. Unless this trauma is acknowledged and worked through, the divorced individual will have a difficult time functioning in a healthy and productive manner. Unfortunately today, with the increased acceptance of divorce, we find a decrease in concern for the devastating effects that divorce can have on peoples' lives. As one columnist observed, we no longer ostracize those who divorce. Now we neglect them or expect that they will adjust to their single state immediately.

A man told the story of the death of his marriage. As a young man he had a dream. He always imagined that in addition to a successful career he would marry and settle down with his family in a nice house in the suburbs. By the time he was thirty-five his dream seemed to have come true. When he was confronted with his wife's emotional collapse and her subsequent desire to be free of him, he, too, went into an emotional tailspin. They tried a trial separation, came back together for a while, and finally realized that they could no longer live together. Eventually she obtained a legal divorce, and he lived in a nearby apartment so he would be close to his children. When his wife sold the dream house and moved out of state to "start a new life" he was forced to accept the reality that no matter how much he wanted to be happily married and living in the suburbs, he was not. At forty-five he was a divorced man, living by himself, far away from his younger children. He had gone through all the stages of divorce and at this time was attempting to decide what to do with his life now that the dream had turned into a nightmare. He felt he had lost his ability to dream, yet he didn't want to give up, to lose hope that somehow the dream had been a good one even though it had not worked out for him.

As a Catholic he was concerned about his status within the Church, since participation in the church community had been an important part of his dream. Up until this time involvement in church activities had been one of his major concerns. He was unsure of his position in his parish church now that he was divorced.

Nothing seemed to be right for him. He worried about his children. He loved them and was anxious about how to maintain some ties with them. The arrival of the divorce decree on the day he had one of the most challenging meetings of his career shattered him. He could easily have lost his job except his employer, conscious of the depression he was experiencing, exerted just enough pressure to entice him to resume functioning on the job. The man realized that the failure of the marriage was partially his fault; but at this time, he had to accept that there was nothing he could do to rectify the past errors. His guilt feelings were, at times, over-powering; and he was quite frightened whenever he tried to think of the future.

Like other divorced persons he, unconsciously, had gone through all the stages of grief. At first he denied that there was a problem in the marriage that could not be worked out. When his wife left the first time he was bitter about the situation of women in today's world that would make her think she could walk out on him. Then he bargained with her to come back, hoping to work things out. Finally, as he began to function at work, he moved into a period of resignation, and is now trying to build a new life where he can accept the reality of the failure of the marriage, perhaps learn from reflection on what went wrong, and move ahead as best he can.

As long as he remains single he is free to be an active participant in his local church. Problems would occur if, in trying to rebuild his life, he wishes to remarry. It is possible that either he or his former wife could apply for an annulment, and if it is granted they would both be free to remarry; but, at the present time, when the annulment process seems so mysterious, the divorced person still feels a stigma in many church-related activities. In addition, even if he were to receive an annulment, he would still have to cope with the trauma of the ending of his marriage. Though the annulment might free him to remarry, it does not wipe out the fact that he had been married for almost twenty years.

In addition to demonstrating the various stages of grief experienced by a divorced individual, this man is a concrete example of the various dimensions of divorce which are discussed in literature on the subject. The emotional breakup of the marriage began long before the actual end of the union, yet the emotional dimension of divorce is one aspect that continues throughout all the stages of divorce even into the period of readjustment. In his case there had been quite a long period of discontent on his wife's part before she confronted him with the request for a divorce. For some couples this is often the period where they seek counseling, and sometimes a reconciliation is achieved, but in many cases the attempt to save the marriage occurs after the relationship is damaged irrevocably. It is during the initial stage of this emotional divorce that the couple dies to each other, and outside observers often comment: "If only they would have worked a little harder." What the observer fails to realize is that by the time of divorce the marriage partners are incapable of giving each other the emotional support they had originally pledged, and this void in their relationship makes it impossible for them to take the steps necessary to work out a harmonious relationship. Although the emotional bond is broken, it was an important part of the individual's life and will have an effect on how he or she faces the future.

There are also the legal aspects of divorce which, depending on where one lives can be complex or simple. Although the legal restrictions against divorce have lessened as the state feels it has less stake in marriage, there still is a legal process. As the man in our example shows, the reminder of an inability to honor a legal contract is another unpleasant dimension of divorce. Closely tied into the legal dimension of divorce is the economic aspect. Although in advanced technological societies there is less need for a woman to continue to depend on her former husband for economic support, this does not mean that the economic tie of marriage is easily broken. A couple shares a style of living and material possessions when they are married, and the splitting up of a household is a reminder that one other dimension of their life together is ending. In those cases where a wife, who is unskilled, must seek a job to support herself or where a husband must continue to support his children and maintain his own apartment, the economic break can constitute a great hardship. Given the complications of the economic tie of marriage, a settlement of economic issues often must be worked out in the legal divorce.

The aspect of divorce which is often the most perplexing for that half of the divorcing population which has children is the parental dimension. Unfortuantely, when both parents are experiencing great emotional stress they often are unable to consider the best interest of their children. The use of a child to get even with the other spouse is an all too common occurrence, even among parents who are attempting to be conscious of the needs of the children. And when all other reminders of the marital union begin to fade from one's mind the children continue to bring back memories of the former relationship.

Though the partners may cease to be spouse to each other, they continue to have a link through the child, a link that is fraught with potential for trouble. Given the guilt that can accumulate when a parent considers the difficulties he has created for his child, it is easy for him to begin to imagine that every crisis of growing up is a result of the fact that he has been unable to maintain a complete family. The parent who obtains custody of the child has the burdens of a single parent, and the one who leaves the family has the guilt of being an absent parent. Even when the parent has been uninterested in the parental role while a member of the family, the inability to assume this task, except at appointed times, causes great hardship for the parent as well as the child. The complications of the parental dimension of divorce are often the greatest obstacle to adjustment after a divorce.

In addition to one's role as a parent undergoing change, the divorced person must also consider her role in the larger community. Parents, other members of the extended family, friends, business associates, and members of any other communities to which the partners belong individually or as a couple are a reminder of the community dimension of divorce. The reactions of persons in these groups vary depending on their acceptance of divorce. So, in a Catholic family the mother of a divorced woman refuses to even acknowledge that the marriage has ended and continues to talk as if her daughter still were married. An aunt refuses to invite a remarried neice to a family wedding. The parents of a man who has been deserted by his wife accuse him of forcing her to leave, though it is obvious that the woman had great emotional problems even prior to the marriage. The parish can't decide whether to allow a divorced woman to be active in a CCD program for fear that it might upset some of the more conservative parishioners. The company officers are all family men who have some misgivings about divorce; and a man feels their disapproval, though unspoken, might ruin his chances for promotion. Even those who are accepting of divorce, at times, react in a manner which indicates its unpleasantness.

Friends don't know which one of a couple to invite to a party, so they invite neither. Other acquaintances try to take advantage of the sexual vulnerability of the newly divorced person. Still others, who would like to be supportive, are uncertain how to respond, so they avoid the subject if they do encounter the divorced friend. Even in the new communities one moves into, the fact that one is divorced will influence, in varying degrees, one's identity in a group.

The issue of a person's identity highlights the significance of the psychological dimension of divorce. The marriage commitment includes an agreement of mutual support as the partners progress through the various stages of adult life. When marriages fail it is usually because one or both partners are unwilling or unable to honor this commitment. But the partners still have developed patterns of interaction which will need to be altered once the relationship is ended. The psychological dependency which develops in a marriage, even when it is a neurotic dependency, become so familiar that an individual must adjust to life without these patterns. Despite the relief that some individuals may feel at the termination of an unhappy relationship they might find themselves depressed at the loneliness of being single after having been part of a couple. The struggle to find oneself in the midst of the trauma of divorce is important for a person who wants to overcome its debilitating effects.

Obviously, not every divorcing person is conscious of the various stages and dimensions of divorce identified here, but the literature on divorce indicates that far from the popular image of the carefree divorcee turning into a swinging single, divorced individuals face a difficult task as they adjust to life. Given the increased life-span of modern technological societies, a person who divorces at 25 faces over forty years of life after the end of a marriage; and one, who divorces after 20 years of marriage, still looks forward to 20 or 30 years of life. Statistics indicate that most people who divorce remarry, at least after a first divorce, which is not surprising, given the human desire for companionship and the life expectancy rate in advanced societies.[3] Acknowledging and dealing with the stages and dimensions of divorce is crucial for someone who hopes to avoid the mistakes of the first marriage the second time.

Now that we have examined divorce, not as an abstract concept, but as a concrete experience, and have seen that divorced persons have many needs which currently are not being met by our society, we need to examine the Church teaching on divorce and the present Church practices regarding the status of divorced Catholics. A new perspective on divorce should show how the Church can remain true to its task to continue the teachings of Jesus and also respond to the needs of church members.

II

LET NO MAN PUT ASUNDER

Prior to the Second Vatican Council Catholics had a clear understanding of the Church teaching on divorce. As stated in *The Sacrament of Matrimony: A Dogmatic Study,*[4] "The Catholic Church teaches that divorce is contrary to the natural law and the divine positive law, and that marriage is indissoluble both by reason of the natural law and the divine positive law." Since the Church was considered incapable of error and what the Church taught was a continuation of what Jesus taught, Catholics were convinced of the continuity of the prohibition of divorce from the time of Christ until the 20th century. A marriage between two Christians contracted in a Church ceremony and then consumated was a sacrament and could not be ended, or if ended civilly neither partner was free to remarry while the spouse was still living.

However, if the couple was married by a justice of the peace or if one of the partners was not a baptized Christian, the marriage was not a sacrament, and it might be possible for the partners to divorce and later enter a sacramental marriage. In addition, annulments were allowed in certain instances, but the general understanding of annulments was that they were available for those who could "pay." When a prominent movie actress married her third husband in a Church wedding, this belief was reinforced. Then those who understood the workings of canon law would be busy explaining impediments to a valid marriage or the Pauline Privilege or the Privilege of the Faith. None of these exceptions were seen as compromising the absolute prohibition of divorce and remarriage.

The rigidity of the Church's stand was evidenced when a divorced and remarried relative was not allowed to be a godparent to a niece, or a friend's confirmation sponsor, or a bridesmaid at a sister's wedding, or in the United States, where excommunication was applied until as recently as 1977, was denied a Catholic burial. Though we had sympathy for these individuals we accepted the fact that the Church was continuing the teaching of Jesus, and that the prohibition of divorce and remarriage was a direct command from Him.

When the Second Vatican Council encouraged widespread study of Scripture and discussions developed among theologians on the evolving character of Church doctrine, Catholics began to examine the Church teaching on divorce and discover that the position has not been as univocal as we had previously believed.

The first step in an examination of the history of a Church teaching is a review of the Scriptural sources. The indissolubility of marriage is treated in five New Testament passages. These are Mark 10:2-10; Luke 16:18; Matthew 5:31-32; Matthew 19:3-12; and I Corinthians 7:10-15.

These five passages, which have their roots in the interpretation Jesus puts on Genesis 1:27 and 2:22-24 have been the object of continual interpretation in every generation since the Apostolic era. Undoubtedly some of the confusion on the correct interpretation of these scriptural passages has been caused by the particular problems connected with divorce in each of these periods. In addition there has been so much discussion of these passages that eventually the various theories seemed to rob the original instruction of any meaning.

However, recent biblical scholarship, through analysis of the ways in which a saying of Jesus was included in the New Testament writings by the early Church, leans rather heavily in the direction of the theory that except for Paul, and perhaps the two passages in Matthew, the teaching of Jesus on the issue is quite clear. He who divorces his wife and marries another commits adultery.

The formula in Mark and Luke, which admits of no exception, and which most interpreters accept as the more original form is definitely contrary to the teachings of the time and place of Jesus and the early Church. In Judaism there was a controversy on divorce which centered around the debate between the rabinnical school of Hillel which permitted divorce for any transgression commited by the wife against the husband and the school of Shammai which only allowed divorce on the grounds of adultery, (though even here there is some discussion that adultery also included other behavior which made life with one's wife unbearable.) In Jewish culture there was no provision for the wife to divorce her husband, but the divorced woman was free to remarry. But she could never return to her first husband, even after the death of her second husband. Roman law at the time differed in allowing the wife to divorce her husband which probably accounts for Mark's reference to the "woman who divorces her husband" (Mark 10:12).

The exception clauses in Matthew have been the cause of much controversy. *Porneia,* which has been translated as fornication, or adultery, or unchastity or lewd conduct is thought by some to simply refer to an illicit union of concubinage, which would make the marriage a marriage in appearance only and thereby rule out any exception to divorce in the gospels. Other biblical scholars consider it possible that Matthew, the last of the synoptic gospels in its present form, encountered problems in his community's acceptance of the apodictic prohibition of divorce, and, like Paul, allowed for an exception. So the controversy continues on a correct Matthean interpretation.

Yet it is still reasonable to conclude, when we include Paul's account in I Corinthians, that Jesus forbade divorce, but in at least one instance Paul found it necessary to make an exception. Paul's authority for allowing an exception comes as he puts it because, "I think I have the Spirit of God" (I Cor. 7:40). The exception was allowed because, "God has called you to a life of peace" (I Cor. 7:16). Thus it is possible to find what appears to be an absolute prohibition by Jesus modified to meet the needs of his followers which perhaps had not been envisioned at the time the original discourse on divorce took place.

From this scriptural background the Church, since the earliest times has upheld the command of Jesus, but developed provisions for dealing with exceptions. The command of Jesus demands that his followers recognize the importance of a lasting marital union, yet it does not specify a policy for a community of Christians some of whom will find themselves unable to remain in a specific life-long marital relationship. So we look in vain for scriptural support for the absolute indissolubility of *only* valid marriages between two baptized Christians who have consumated that union through one act of intercourse, as we also do not find stipulations of impediments or penalties, or talk of marriage contracts or defect of form or any other of the rules and regulations which are part of the present Church position on divorce and remarriage. All of these developed in the tradition of the Church which needs to be examined to determine if the Church position has been univocal in its prohibition of divorce and remarriage.

A review of the fathers of the Church, the teachings of the popes and councils, the predominant theological positions, and the practice of the faithful demonstrates how the present legalistic understanding of marriage as contract developed.[5]

The Church in all ages has taught that the indissolubility of marriage is an ideal, a goal to be sought after and desired, even though in practice, at various times, exceptions have been made. For the first thousand years of church history the indissolubility of *all* marriages was taught as an ideal. In practice in the East, and at some times in the West, there were exceptions. From the 4th to the 6th century imperial legislation allowing divorce existed alongside the conviction of Jerome, Ambrose, and Augustine that remarriage is invalid as long as the other partner is alive. From the 6th century on, the East recognized that the Church can and does dissolve sacramental marriages, at least in the case of adultery. During this same time, when periods of laxity in practice mingled with teaching of the Christian ideal, we find little attempt to designate a particular doctrine or identify the sacramental character of marriage.

With the advent of the feudal system the Church became responsible for both the sacramental and civil legislation of marriage, and the bishops in the West were called upon to decide the solution to problem marriages. This was the beginning of a continuous development of a legalistic understanding of marriage and divorce which had its basis in various decrees and decisions of previous popes and councils. But there was little attempt to develop a vital theology of the sacramentality of marriage. As the example of the debate between the Bologna school and the Paris school on the necessity of carnal relations to form the matrimonial bond indicates, papal decisions on what constitutes a valid marriage contract had a vast influence on the direction of the theology of marriage. The legalistic bent, begun at that time, persists until the present day.

The Council of Trent, in opposing the teachings of the Reformers, reasserted the sacramental character of marriage as well as its indissolubility, but the emphasis then and now still is of a highly legalistic nature. After the Council of Trent reaffirmed the indissolubility of marriage, the popes expanded their power to dissolve marriages through the privilege of the faith by responding to needs in missionary countries, and the Pauline privilege was increasingly applied to exceptions to the ideal of indissolubility.

Thus we see that although the Church has always taught the ideal of marriage indissolubility as pronounced by Jesus, it continually found it necessary, sometimes to a greater or lesser degree to respond to specific problems of a time or place and acknowledge exceptions which allow for divorce and remarriage. Before proposing a new perspective on divorce we will examine the present Church treatment of exceptions to the ideal.

III

THE CHURCH PUTS ASUNDER

The interpretation of Jesus' prohibition of divorce by successive generations of theologians and canon lawyers has led us to the present situation in the Catholic Church where decisions as to whether a man and woman may end one marriage and enter another are made by tribunals. Tribunals are judicial agencies of a diocese which are charged with safeguarding the rights of individuals as members of the Church as well as safeguarding the observance of divine and ecclesiastical law. At the present time the main focus of tribunals is on the determination of the status of those persons who want to marry within the Catholic Church.

The justification for such marriage tribunals comes from the need for a human organization, which has the responsibility of continuing the mission of Jesus Christ, to establish ordinances which assure the rights, privilege and obligations of its members. In the area of marriage the tribunal attempts to help individual Christians determine if they are free to marry within the norms established by the Church as it interprets the will of Christ found in the Scriptures.

As the number of Catholics who seek divorce increases, the concern for the status of those who divorce and remarry has become an important pastoral priority. Since the theology of marriage has been deficient, the solution to this dilemma has been left to canon lawyers, who are attempting to identify what makes a legal marriage contract within the Catholic Church, and, on this basis, to nullify many marriages which do not meet the legal criteria.

Many of the impediments which render a Catholic marriage invalid have been acknowledged in the past, but it is only in the last decade and a half that there has been an extension of the understanding of impediments to include psychological incompatibility. Not all canon lawyers are in agreement with the validity of the widening interpretation of this impediment, but in the late 1970s there was an increased use of this approach to ending a marriage within the Catholic Church. In those dioceses where there are sufficient tribunal personnel more and more marriages are being declared null and the marriage partners are free to remarry, or, if already remarried, are allowed to participate, once again, in the sacramental life of the Church. The growing rate of annulments has led some to claim that the annulment process is simply a Catholic approach to allowing divorce while refusing to acknowledge this due to previous Church teaching.

Since there is widespread confusion concerning marriage tribunals, marriage dissolutions and annulments, it is necessary to investigate the function of this body of the diocesan church and to evaluate this perspective on divorce. We will consider the positive and negative aspects of tribunals as we seek to determine the validity of this response to divorced Catholics in a modern technological society.

The marriage tribunal is charged with determining whether or not a marriage may be dissolved or annulled. There are three instances where the Church claims the power to dissolve valid marriages. These are in cases of ratified non-consumated marriages, cases of the Pauline Privilege and those associated with the Privilege of the Faith (also known as the Petrine Privilege). In all three instances the tribunals base their authority on an interpretation of an exception to the apodictic command of Jesus.

Canon law states that a marriage between two baptized persons, or between a baptized and non-baptized person which has never been consummated through sexual intercourse can be dissolved automatically by law through solemn religious profession or by a dispensation from the Holy See if this is sought for just cause by either party. Since it is required that proof be supplied and that the case be sent to Rome for final decision, if non-consumation is thought to be an indication of other impediments tribunals often will seek to nullify the marriage (which can be done at the diocesan level).

St. Paul's exception has, after various interpretations, become the basis for the tribunal power to dissolve a legitimate marriage between two unbaptized persons, even when consumated. Requirements are: 1) Both partners to the original marriage must have been unbaptized at the time of marriage and have remained unbaptized throughout the entire marriage; 2) the petitioner (one of the unbaptized marriage partners) must sincerely desire to be baptized; 3) the respondent (the other unbaptized partner) must be asked if he or she wishes to be baptized or live peacefully with the petitioner. The marriage is dissolved only when the petitioner, having been baptized, enters into a second marriage in the Church. Pastoral ministers are counselled not to baptize the petitioner until a Decree is issued by the Ordinary. This latter point is heavily emphasized since the petitioner must remain unbaptized while requesting this privilege.

The Privilege of the Faith is a petition which is sent to the Holy Father requesting that he dissolve a marriage in which at least one person is unbaptized. This also can be applied in cases of mixed marriage between a Catholic and non-baptized person performed with a dispensation from disparity of the faith. The serious reason of favoring the faith for which a marriage is thus dissolved means that the petitioner sincerely wishes to become a Catholic, or if he or she does not wish to convert, wishes to marry a Catholic who wishes to continue to live his or her baptismal commitment. It also refers to a Catholic from a previous valid, but non-sacramental marriage who now wishes to enter into a sacramental marriage. In all cases neither the petitioner nor the party in the new marriage can be the cause of the breakup of the marriage to be dissolved. This particular petition goes to Rome, and the former marriage is dissolved at the time the Holy Father decrees it to be. Again the petitioner is not baptized until the decree is handed down.

In all three cases a valid marriage has taken place, but the Church has assumed the power to put asunder the former marriage and permit another marriage. A declaration of nullity or an annulment is different in that, although a marriage ceremony has taken place, that attempt at marriage was invalid and a true marriage never existed. The decree of annulment does not, from the Canon Law perspective, terminate an existing marriage. It declares that a marriage never existed. In other words, the marriage was never a valid, sacramental union.

A common reason for nullifying marriages involving Catholics is the failure to celebrate the wedding according to canonical form, known as the defect of form. We have all heard the comment, "They'd be better off getting married by a justice of the peace," applied to a couple that seem obviously mismatched. "That way they can always get married later to someone else in the Church." Another possible defect occurs and renders a marriage invalid when a previous marriage bond still exists. This often occurs when there have been a series of marriages involving baptized and unbaptized individuals married outside the Catholic Church. Other less frequently encountered conditions, which often were more regular in previous periods are: age of male under 16 and female under 14; physical impotency, sacred orders, solemn vows, abduction, crimes, consanguinity, affinity, public propriety, and spiritual relationship through baptism.

The most frequent case of annulment petitions accounting for the increase in annulments at the present time, however, is in the category of formal annulments. In this case the intention or the capabilities of one or both of the parties at the time of the marriage are called into question.

Marriage, according to canon law, is constituted by the consent of persons who are capable by law of marriage. When two people marry, if they are of mature age, it is assumed that they intend a life-long union where they will remain faithful to each other and open to having children and that they are capable of making and fulfilling these promises. Canon lawyers accept that this assumption is subject to contrary proof. The Fornal Annulment Process of the marriage tribunal allows that if contrary proof is demonstrated a marriage may be declared null from the beginning, giving the partners the right to marry validly at some other time.

According to canon law, then, one must intend marriage and all its essentials to marry validly. The annulment does not deny that a real relationship existed, nor does it say that there was deliberate intent to deceive at the time of marriage. Instead it indicates that a marriage fell short of one of the elements seen as essential for a binding union. Circumstances which would indicate a lack of essentials include exclusion of life-long commitment, of children or of fidelity. In addition, force or fear at the time of the wedding, undue pressure from premarital pregnancy, severe immaturity, mental illness, or an inability to exercise good judgement could render a marriage contract invalid. Also a person who is suffering from physical or psychic impotency, irresponsibility, alcoholism or drug abuse, homosexuality or personality disorders may be incapable of carrying out the essential duties and obligations of marriage.

In any formal annulment process an exclusion, incapacity, or defect must be proven to have existed prior to the marriage ceremony so that it could be said that, even though not fully understood, the person was incapable of living out the essentials of marriage at the time of the wedding. In such a situation the person also would be incapable of giving correct assent. Though the behavior which would allow an annulment may not have surfaced before the wedding, tribunal personnel are beginning to listen to the argument that personality traits do not simply appear. Behavior after the wedding had roots prior to the ceremony, and possibly could affect a person's intentions and capacity to agree to the contract.

Since there are probably few marriages, especially of people in their teens and early twenties, where both partners have all the necessary intentions and capabilities, it is little wonder that we have an increase in the number of appeals to and favorable decisions granted by the marriage tribunals. A number of observers of the tribunal process feel that there are very few marriages which could pass the demand that the partners be mature and stable and psychologically able to enter into a binding union with the specific other they married at the time of the marriage ceremony. These critics maintain that what we have, in effect is Catholic divorce.

Those partners who manage to grow in their marriage, or who do not experience the traumas which lead others to divorce, might have been no more validly married at the time of their wedding; but they have not attempted divorce, so they have not subjected their marriage to the scrutiny that the annulment procedure requires. It is only those couples who find themselves in a situation where they want to end the marriage who begin to consider how their marriage might not have been valid, and many do this only if they are considering remarrying and want to do so within the Church.

Since, at the present time, the tribunal is the primary way in which Catholics who divorce and are remarried, or who seek to remarry, may do so and keep their religious affiliation, it is important to evaluate the tribunal process to determine if this process should be expanded or if some alternative approach would be more responsive to the needs of people at the present time.

The most positive feature of the marriage tribunal today is that it is the chief means available to divorced and remarried Catholics who wish to maintain a status within the Church. As one woman, whose husband left her during one of his many alcoholic bouts and married at least two more times, said: "One divorce is enough for me. I want to stay united with my Church." For those who have continued an interest in their religion, even though divorce has cut them off from sacramental participation, the annulment procedure is a welcome way to reestablish an important tie in their lives.

Another value of the formal annulment process is the assistance it offers the person seeking the annulment, and often the other spouse, in evaluating the reasons why the first marriage decision was not able to sustain a lifelong union. The process of examining the past and realizing that you chose a certain mate to escape from your parents, or to avoid dealing with an identity crisis, or because you wanted to save the person from alcohol is a painful process because it necessitates reviewing parts of life which most of us feel are best left untouched. But, in fact, if these issues can be faced and understood the individual will be equipped with the means for avoiding similar mistakes in the choice of another partner. For the individual who has not already entered into a second marriage or chosen another partner, the formal annulment process can assist as he or she seeks to restructure his or her life. In some instances the annulment is granted with a recommendation encouraging counseling to further assist in this restructuring, while in other cases a prohibition actually blocks remarriage within the Church unless the person has received adequate counseling.

A side effect of the tribunal process, which is beneficial to the Church, is the increase of consciousness of tribunal personnel regarding the problems of divorced Catholics. Even though their focus is primarily that of canon law, many of these men are attempting to do whatever is legally possible to relieve the sufferings of divorced Catholics. They have helped to raise the consciousness of theologians and Church officials to the pastoral problems of divorce and remarriage.

The most negative aspect of the tribunal is its legalistic framework. Marriage is viewed as a contract which, when certain specifics are lacking, is not legally binding, and therefore, can be broken. For many Catholics in a post-Vatican II Church, the paternalism of this legalistic approach to both Church and sacrament is no longer acceptable. The guidelines for processing marriage cases in one large archdiocese in the United States cautions, *"Please remember that this booklet is not designed for the use of your parishioners."* The legalistic and paternalistic mentality which would make this suggestion for a booklet that contains nothing more than an explanation of the rationale for the various types of dissolutions and annulments, the fees charged, and the procedures to be followed by parish priests, is a mentality which retains many aspects of pre-Vatican II ecclesiology. It alienates the sophisticated and increasingly better-educated Catholic, and tends to frighten those who do not understand the workings of the Church.

Another negative feature of the tribunal approach is tied into the previous legalistic style which gives the tribunal a very mysterious image. As a function of the diocesan church which is executed away from the parish community, and seldom, if ever, discussed outside of instances where a person needs to make use of it, the tribunal and its work are misunderstood by most Catholics. And warnings not to let parishioners see guidelines for the tribunal reinforce its mysterious and secretive impression.

Many priests are unaware of the new guidelines and are ill-equipped to counsel their parishioners when they seek advice. One deserted wife was advised to go home and pray: "Every marriage has its troubles. Yours will work out I'm sure, my dear." If this person, and others like her, are aware of the tribunal process, they would be able to seek help through some other avenue; but, if not, they would be faced with the dilemma of being cut off from their religious community.

In one case a woman married an immature young man when she was eighteen years old. After bearing six children during which time he repeatedly left her, she finally refused to allow him to return. Some 15 years later she married a Catholic man, who was free to marry; but due to her prior Catholic marriage they were not allowed to be married within the Church. When the second marriage was nearing its twentieth anniversary she was seriously ill in the hospital. A young priest visited her, heard her confession, brought her communion, and promised to see if he could straighten out her status in the Church. For the twenty years of her second marriage both she and her husband attended Mass each Sunday, contributed to their church and followed the other rules of the Church. Unfortunately, the young priest left his ministry, and this woman, who had no more than a grammar school education did not know where to go for assistance. Eventually she and her husband sought the advice of a priest friend of his, an oldtimer who told them he would look into the new procedures for them, but they must agree to live as brother and sister until an annulment could be obtained. The couple, now in their late sixties were, understandably, insulted by the treatment they received.

Other "horror" stories about the annulment process abound. Spouses of petitioners often are incensed that their former marriage partner would attempt to maintain that their marriage had never existed and they are eager to portray the entire annulment process in a bad light. It is little wonder that most Catholics are skeptical about annulments.

Another negative feature of the tribunal is that, although the process may assist the persons involved in assessing past mistakes, the request for annulment often comes too late to be of real assistance. The majority of annulment requests are made either after a second marriage has been contracted or once a person has already chosen a second partner. Once a choice has been made it is difficult to exercise objectivity in evaluating the reasons for the choice.

Finally, it is obvious that more and more people are rejecting those aspects of the Church which represent the heirarchial model of Christian community. The formal annulment procedure offers Catholics who are concerned about the approval of higher authorities an opportunity to remain in the Church even though they have divorced and remarried; but it is questionable how long this legal approach will be acceptable to young lay people and clergy who have been raised in a Church which emphasizes personal responsibility for moral decisions and the importance of a freely chosen religious commitment. In a survey of opinions of Chicago Catholics only 34 percent of those under age 30 who receive communion weekly and pray daily disapprove of divorce as opposed to 43 percent of those over 30. In a survey of the entire United States Catholic population the difference in age groups was not as significant (44 percent of those under 30 and 45 percent of those over 30), but there is still a greater percentage of Catholics who approve of divorce than those who disapprove.[6]

In a 1978 survey of hundreds of American parishes, *U.S. Catholic* reported that 42 percent of the pastoral ministers responded that they "knew some members in the parish who are in illicit Catholic marriages and receive communion."[7] Some of these are, more than likely, making use of the internal forum or good faith solution to problem marriages. This approach maintains that those who are in their present marriages in sincere good faith may be allowed to receive the sacraments as a matter of conscience even though their status is not officially recognized by the Church. As the annulment process comes under greater scrutiny, and more people begin to question whether or not it is simply Catholic divorce, the number of internal forum solutions will undoubtedly increase. Unfortunately, at the present time, this resolution of a divorce and remarriage problem does not challenge the wider community to come to grips with the need for a Catholic perspective on divorce. In most instances, the other members of the community are unaware of the use of the internal forum solution.

So, although at the present time, the marriage tribunal is responding to the immediate need of a divorced or remarried Catholic who wishes to maintain an active status within the Church, it does not meet the greater need of the Church to have a vital theology of marriage which recognizes that some marriages in a modern technological society are not and never could be sacraments. Not because these marriages lack the legal requirements for a contract (which they might), but because the partners lack the ability to enter into a sacramental relationship. A Catholic perspective on divorce developed out of a sacramental understanding of marriage is needed if the Church hopes to present a Christian response to the needs of its suffering members while at the same time continuing to teach the importance of the indissolubility of marriage.

IV

TO LIVE IN PEACE

According to the teaching of Jesus, God ordained from the beginning that a man should leave mother and father and cling to his wife so the "two would become one flesh." Two becoming one flesh has given rise to biblical images of the marriage relationship being comparable to the relationship of Yahweh and his people and Christ and the Church. In other words, marriage, which is a manifold symbol has been interpreted by both Old and New Testament writers as a religious symbol. For a symbol to continue its symbolic character and be a sacrament carrying on the mystery of Christ and the Church in the present day it is necessary that it have a certain connection between it and the event of Jesus which it wants to represent. If the present event participates in the symbol it also participates in the grace to continue the symbol in the present time, but in order to participate in the symbol there must be, at least, an openness to being the continuation of the symbol.

Marriage today continues to call forth a fidelity and love which would somehow represent the mystery of Christ and the Church because it is within a marriage relationship that most people have the opportunity to develop their capacity for intimacy which in turn enables them to move through the succeeding crises of adult growth and development. Both the individual who enters into a marriage and the society as a whole need a vision of marriage which articulates the importance of life-long love and fidelity.

When we see the sacramental nature of marriage in an advanced technological society being related to the capacity of the couple to actualize their potential for intimacy we begin to appreciate the problems which some couples experience in achieving a sacramental marriage.

A Catholic perspective on divorce which develops out of this understanding of the sacramentality of marriage recognizes that just as individuals in advanced societies are free to choose to marry the person they love, they are free to marry the wrong person or to marry before they are secure enough in their own identities to be able to risk intimacy with another. Marriages today are free to fail to be a symbol of the relationship of Christ and the Church.

A Catholic response to the situation of those who fail to be the symbol, because either one or both partners is unwilling or unable to work at developing their capacity for intimacy, must understand the situation of divorce and respond to the individuals involved from a Christian perspective. As noted in our examination of the stages and dimensions of divorce, the divorced person in an advanced society has a considerable span of life after a divorce. Since the practice of previous times of returning to the family of birth after a divorce is no longer an option for most divorced individuals, a Catholic perspective must also consider the status of those persons who remarry after divorce.

St. Paul allowed an exception to the command of Jesus because God calls us to live in peace. Given the human need for companionship and the loneliness of an *enforced* single state, we must question the position that denies active church membership to divorced and remarried Catholics. The position becomes more untenable when we observe that a Catholic who made a wrong marriage choice yet was married to another Christian in a church wedding is forbidden to remarry, while a Catholic who married her wrong choice before a justice of the peace is free, at a later time, to remarry and remain active in the Church. The Church response to these persons should be one which encourages those who have made a mistake in their first marriage choice to develop the capacity to live in peace if they choose to enter a second marriage.

The tradition of the Eastern Church on

divorce and remarriage gives some hints of how this practice does not deny the Church teaching on the indissolubility of marriage. There, in certain concrete situations the Church recognizes that due to sin, ignorance, lack of faith and love, selfishness, or passion, marriages dissolve. The Church does not dissolve the marriage. By the time the situation reaches a resolution in actual divorce, the Church recognizes that it is already dissolved, and allows those partners who enter into a second marriage to remain in the Church community. It does not, however, recognize in the second marriage the same sacramental nature as the first. Yet since the stipulation for the second marriage to be accepted is that it allows the person to live a Christian life there is room for further elaboration of the possibility of a second marriage being sacramental. As our earlier reference to the woman who was in her second marriage for over twenty years indicates, it is possible for these unions to be recognized as signs of faithfulness and love which could symbolize the love of Christ and the Church.

Obviously, such a position raises problems. Aren't there some Catholics who would choose to enter a second marriage in the Church only for the prestige of a church wedding? Won't some Catholics walk out on their responsibilities if they know the Church accepts divorce and remarriage? Aren't there Catholics who will give insufficient thought to the seriousness of their marriage choices if they know they can remarry? The answer to all of these is, yes, but there are Catholics who are doing these things now and who are supported in their behavior by the manner in which marriages are annulled and dissolved at the present time.

The annulment procedure allows divorced Catholics to remarry if they lacked the intention or the capability to enter into a valid contract at the time they married. Divorce and remarriage when a marriage lacked the capacity to be a sacramental, covenant relationship recognizes that some individuals are unwilling or unable to enter into an intimacy relationship with each other, but does not rule out the possibility that at some other time a person might be able to exercise her capacity for intimacy in such a way that the Church could recognize this as a sign of the mystery of Christ and the Church. Though the end result of the legalistic and sacramental understandings of marriage applied to the situation of divorce is the same (divorced Catholics are allowed to remarry and retain their status as members of the community), the sacramental approach demands much greater responsibility on the part of the individual and the local church both for maintaining the importance of the marriage bond and for assisting those who divorce to recapture their ability to live in peace, either by remaining in the single state or entering into a second marriage.

Pastoral reform in the area of divorce should move away from the legalistic understanding of marriage and divorce which characterizes the marriage tribunal and call for a pastoral theology which articulates a deepened understanding of the nature of sacramental marriage in our contemporary world. This approach to pastoral theology requires that a theology of marriage have its impetus, as well as its implementation, at the level of the local parish, be that a geographical or a special interest group community. If we apply the principle of subsidiarity to the issue of divorce both at the level of developing policy and of executing it we begin the process of including the experience of community members in the formulation of a Catholic perspective.

Any perspective on divorce developed at the local level would need to be informed by and critiqued by the central story of the Christian tradition and should not simply be an attempt by the Catholic Church to identify with the solutions to divorce offered by the contemporary culture. The lack of preparation for marriage in our contemporary world leads many people to make wrong decisions in the choice of a marital partner. This, in turn, increases the possibility of divorce, which even with the Church approval of annulment, is a shattering experience. If the local church community begins to appreciate the problems of divorce it will recognize the importance of better marriage preparation, and it will attempt to develop ways to respond to the needs of those who have lost their ability to dream as a result of a divorce.

When the local parish has the responsibility of marriage education and develops an understanding of how marriage in today's culture is sacramental, there will be little need to prohibit divorced and remarried Catholics from participation in the religious community as an educational deterrent to divorce. If the richness of the possibilities of sacramental marriage are understood, and if couples who are married are able to articulate the ways in which sacramental marriage enriches their lives, the fear that allowing divorced and remarried Catholics to participate in the church will encourage divorce is unfounded. The way will be opened for community members to begin to listen to the problems of those who have not been able to achieve a sacramental marriage and to support and encourage them as they seek to regain the capacity to dream. The parish will begin to practice its religious mission of responding to the needs of individuals by helping them see how their experience can be accepted and managed, or maybe only tolerated, because of its place in the experience of Christ and the Christian tradition. The divorced person needs acceptance, healing and reconciliation, all of which the local church should be prepared to offer.

Although specific approaches to implementing this sacramental vision of marriage and the community response to those who have not been able to achieve this would differ from place to place, it does not seem necessary to retain the legalistic approach of the tribunal. Some form of the good faith approach which recognizes that the Christian community wants marriage to be sacramental, but acknowledges that the individual is the best person to judge whether the union they are in is so intolerable that it cannot be sustained would seem more desirable. Once a union has been broken the partners have a responsibility to determine why they were unsuccessful before seeking to attempt a second marriage. The local church might assist in the process of adjustment and the choice of a second mate when that occurs, but it does not need to do this in the role of judge. Rather it should provide the incentive to motivate a divorced Catholic, who is considering remarriage, to choose more wisely the second time.

Undoubtedly just as many marriages continue which, according to canon law standards, are not valid marriages, there will be marriages that do not end when a couple fails to develop intimacy. Perhaps neither partner in this type of relationship wants or needs intimacy and is not upset by the lack of it. Or other external pressures will keep a couple, who do not feel they have a sacramental union, together. This does not mean that a couple who finds their relationship intolerable should be forced to either remain together or the partners not seek another intimate relationship if they want to remain joined to the Christian community. Paul taught that God wants us to live in peace. Since marriage in our present society is a major determiner of its partners ability to live in peace a marital union which denies this ability cannot be considered sacramental.

In concluding this review of the factors which should be considered when developing a Catholic perspective on divorce, we acknowledge that in advanced technological societies people will continue to make wrong choices when they marry, to divorce, to suffer the pain and suffering of the loss of a dream, and then to attempt to regain hope in a second marriage. Our examination of the trauma of divorce indicates that the Catholic community should exert great energy in developing an understanding of the sacramental nature of marriage which will encourage better marital choices. We also see the need for the community to be open to assisting divorced persons at all the stages of divorce and during the readjustment period after divorce. Although the Church has an obligation to carry out the command of Jesus to teach the indissolubility of marriage, we have the example of Paul and the Church tradition which has made exception in specific cases. If we apply the rationale for Paul's exception to the case of divorce and remarriage in the contemporary world we find the marriage tribunal's implementation of canon law's understanding of marriage to be lacking in its ability to identify the sacramental dimension of marriage.

The sacramental character of marriage offers us an approach to a new perspective on divorce which eliminates the fear that a development of church teaching on divorce means that the Church errs and fails to teach the message of Jesus. In a people of God perspective on divorce we seek to find a Christian response, through a variety of approaches developed at the local church level, to people who are confronted with the trauma of divorce. We do not seek to save the institution of marriage as an abstract concept that has no relationship to the experience of people. Rather we seek to allow all those who sincerely want to participate in the Christian community to organize their lives in such a manner that they will be free to be active followers of Jesus Christ. The Christian community needs the Aunt Millies of the world and the Aunt Millies need the Christian community. The time has come to begin to allow this reunion to take place within a deepened understanding of the sacramental nature of Christian marriage.

PART ONE NOTES

[1] See A. M. Greeley, *Crisis in the Church: A Study of American Religious Evangelization,* published by Thomas More Press, especially Chapter 1.

[2] For a more detailed discussion of pastoral theology and church reform see, "Pluralism and Church Reform: Pastoral Theology Looks To The Future, in Tracy *et al. Toward Vatican III: The Work That Needs To Be Done* (New York: The Seabury Press) 1978.

[3] Mary Jo Banes, *Here To Stay: American Families in the Twentieth Century* (New York: Basic Books) 1976, pp. 21-36.

[4] C. A. Schleck, *The Sacrament of Marriage: A Dogmatic Study* (Milwaukee: The Bruce Publishing Company) 1964.

[5] For a more detailed study of the historical treatment of divorce in the Church see J. T. Noonan, *Power to Dissolve* (Cambridge, Mass: Harvard University Press) 1972.

[6] Greeley, *op cit* p. 1.24 of manuscript.

[7] Tom Brune, "There's No Such Thing as an Average Parish," *U.S. Catholic,* April, 1978, pp. 6-13.

CATHOLIC PERSPECTIVES

Divorce

PART TWO

by
James Hitchcock

CATHOLICS in America used to be a people noted for their distinctive (some might have said peculiar) way of looking at things, and one of the things which Catholics looked at differently from most people was divorce. In a remarkably short time that has ceased to be the case, and American Catholics increasingly seem to have opinions on moral questions not substantially different from those of non-Catholics. Despite what the media often imply, such a situation is not exactly what the Second Vatican Council intended by renewal.

Scripture scholars are largely agreed about the uncompromising nature of Christ's prohibition of divorce (Mark 10:2-12, Luke 16:18), and the apparent exception for adultery (Matt. 5:31-2, and 19:3-12) is unclear as to precise meaning and possibly a later interpolation. St. Paul's exception in the case of a believer married to an unbeliever (1 Cor. 7:8-16) is thought to represent a softening of Christ's own teaching.[1]

The attempt to revise the Catholic teaching, therefore, does not seem possible on the basis of Scripture, unless the authority of Scripture is simply relativized. One biblical scholar, for example, while admitting the uncompromising nature of Christ's teaching, also dismisses any possibility of "a supposedly divine revealed law." Instead he substitutes a process "of accommodation to circumstances."[2] Another denies that Christ's teaching should be considered a law.[3] What is apparently being proposed is the liberal Protestant idea that, whatever Jesus may have taught or said or whatever may have been the mind of the Scriptures, Christians in each generation are free to reinterpret those words to suit their own situations. There is, finally, no binding authority in matters of morality.

The existence of the Pauline Privilege—the provision whereby the Church undertakes to dissolve existing marriages in which one party is unbaptized—is often cited as demonstrating that doctrine can develop to meet changed historical circumstances. But there is surely an enormous difference between an alleged innovation dating from apostolic times and mentioned in the text of the New Testament itself (the Pauline epistles being, in the opinion of many scholars, even older than the texts of the gospels) and innovations added in later centuries. Finally, however, if the Pauline Privilege is deemed to be an unwarranted modification of the teachings of Christ, true "renewal" would seem to dictate abolishing the privilege, not using it as a basis for indiscriminate further revisions.

The move to persuade the Church to permit divorce rests on the cultural assumptions of modern liberal Protestantism, and this fact is even more obvious in its ecclesiology than in its use of Scripture. Classical Catholic doctrine holds that the Church is the guardian and the interpreter of Divine Revelation, that where the meaning of Christ's teachings is in doubt it is the Church which resolves this doubt, through the guidance of the Holy Spirit. (Where the Church has condoned moral errors, for example, by countenancing slavery, this has been almost always because of an overly permissive acceptance of prevailing cultural norms, not because of excessive strictness.)

Now, however, the Church's refusal to countenance divorce (as well as other popular contemporary practices) has occasioned a sometimes angry denial that the Church has any authority at all. A prominent canon lawyer, for example, dismisses as "a doctrine of the Dark Ages" the idea that the Church possesses truth and can "judge the nations."[4] A theologian postulates that divorced Catholics have "a moral obligation" not to follow the Catholic teaching.[5] Whatever verbal formulas are employed to conceal the fact, what is being asserted is that, on the matter of divorce, the Catholic Church has been in serious error for many centuries. Obviously, if accepted, this assertion has relevance to virtually every other Catholic doctrine.

Those who urge the Church to modify its teachings are thus prepared to pay a very high price for that modification, nothing less than that the Catholic Church should cease to be the Catholic Church, as historically understood. What motivates such a demand? What justifies such a price?

The answer is, allegedly, self-evident—numerous believing Catholics are in fact in violation of the Church's laws concerning marriage. Such people have legitimate claims on the Church for compassion and concern. The existing laws are rigid and inhumane. Such people should not be shut out from the corporate and sacramental life of the Church, should indeed be welcomed and made to feel comfortable.

The cultural accretions which surround contemporary discussions of marriage and divorce are nowhere deeper than at the point of talking about "compassion," "mercy," and "love." Increasingly in recent years, these words have come to be understood in vague, sentimental, and finally un-Christian ways. Their current usage reflects what has been described as a pervasive "therapeutic" mentality—the belief that goodness is equatable with whatever seems to promote the subjective sense of well-being of each individual.[6]

Christian love has traditionally been understood as a cleansing and bracing phenomenon as much as a tender and warming one. The Christian tradition, beginning with Christ, has understood love as that which is truly best for the person who receives it. One implication is that what may prove ultimately best for the person is not necessarily what seems immediately best. Furthermore, love may often be surgical or medicinal in character, bringing pain in order finally to heal. So long as love, and its related virtues of compassion and mercy, is understood primarily as a sympathetic and approving response to the individual's own desires, its true depths will not be comprehended, nor will it have any necessary connection with Christianity. Christ was always loving; He was not by any means always kind.

This does not, of course, mean that a rigorous stand on every question is therefore always the most loving one. It does mean, however, that genuine love and compassion do not necessarily require responding to each person in the way that person desires. Asserting that the Church would show compassion for the divorced by sanctioning remarriage is begging the question: if divorce is contrary to the law of God, then the Church shows compassion precisely by not sanctioning remarriage, because in this way it seeks to motivate the individual to obey God's law. One does not show compassion for an alcoholic by giving him a drink, nor for a racist by agreeing with his bigotry. The question of the sinfulness of divorce must first be confronted before the appropriate pastoral response can be discovered.

The literature which seeks to justify divorce within a Catholic framework is characterized, among other things, by the vagueness of its formulas for anlayzing the breakdown of marriages. A favorite is the mere assertion that a marriage is "dead," which seems a tautology, since by definition those who get divorced regard their marriage as dead (or else want to kill it). A canon lawyer speaks of "the absence of genuineness, empathy or non-possessive caring."[7] Another prominent canon lawyer requires that those involved in marriage continue to "grow" and that "they are substantially attuned to each other psychologically and emotionally."[8] For a Catholic psychiatrist the married couple must "mutually satisfy their needs and in the process continue to grow."[9]

What appears, over and over again in such literature, are verbal formulas which would probably be quite unintelligible to the majority of Catholics presently married, to say nothing of all those generations married in past times. In recent years there has developed, in the affluent Western nations and especially in America, what amounts to an industry catering to the idea of "personal fulfillment." Many people who do not really understand what such incantatory phrases mean nonetheless hold it as a dogma that they deserve such fulfillment and will, given the proper circumstances, find it.

This very small slice of the total human race, the prevailing cultural attitudes of affluent and educated Westerners of the 1970s, has been chosen by the Catholic revisionists as representative of humanity as a whole. The cultural attitudes of such people are permitted to serve as the ultimate criteria by which the rightness or wrongness of religious doctrine is to be judged. What is almost a new language, rarely spoken even a quarter of a century ago, is now the vernacular into which everything must be translated.

Its very vagueness is its undoing, because it is the unusually stupid (or honest) person who, desirous of taking a new spouse, cannot show how "unfulfilling" was the previous union, how inhibiting of spiritual growth. The formulas offered to define a supposedly "dead" marriage can cover everything from a woman who is married to a homicidal alcoholic to one who finds her current husband simply too stodgy and boring.

Consider a common marital situation: the husband is hard-working, conscientious about his familial and social responsibilities, deeply attached to his favored patterns of living (his "ruts"). His wife is his equal in hard work and responsibility but is slightly more sociable and venturesome. He prefers to spend the evening in front of the television; she likes going to parties, films, and restaurants. He is comfortable only with old friends; she likes occasionally to make new ones. On most general questions pertaining to politics, society, or morality both hold to the opinions in which they were raised, although the wife is slightly more ready to hear another point of view. Neither of them is very articulate, the husband preferring to be silent, the wife talking mainly about minor domestic and neighborhood events. They are not good at expressing their feelings and are embarrassed when asked to do so. They were raised, in fact, not to be particularly aware of their feelings and are not good at analyzing them. Sex is occasional and rather perfunctory. They are content with each other, but much of their life can only be described as dull.

Quite possibly the above sketch, or one slightly different, would describe the majority of present marriages, at least of people over the age of forty. It would, quite probably, come close to describing the marriages of the parents of many of the theologians, canonists, and others who now undertake to describe a "healthy" marriage. But what is to be made of such a relationship? Is there really "growth?" Where is the "empathy?" Are either of the partners really "fulfilled?" Ought they, if they knew better, to get divorced and try again?

There seems enormous willingness on the part of the defenders of divorce to put emphasis on certain personal qualities, especially articulateness, which may have little to do with genuine relationships. Consider another familiar pattern of contemporary marriage: husband and wife are initially ecstatic about one another, and highly demonstrative of their mutual affections. Their sex life is active, imaginative, and satisfying. They share dozens of common interests—art, politics, food, nature—and are constantly experiencing the excitement of new discoveries. Scarcely a single thought or feeling, on either side, goes unexpressed, and each makes a strong effort to empathize fully with the feelings of the other. (When the wife becomes a feminist, the husband encourages her and agrees to a new division of domestic responsibilities.)

The latter, clearly, is an ideal marriage. Yet no one is any longer surprised when such ideal relationships break up, and the partners go their separate ways (often remaining "friends"). There is now a generation of married people who enjoy benefits unprecedented in the history of the world—financial security, attractive living conditions, liberal amounts of leisure, "enlightened" attitudes about sex, platoons of experts ready to proffer help on subjects ranging from cooking to psychic anxieties, much premarital experience (sexual, social, and vocational), good educations, interesting occupations. The list could go on and on. Yet it is precisely such people who are getting divorced in ever-increasing numbers and many of whom now question the basic validity of the institution of marriage. Surely the contrast between the two described marriages—stodgy stability versus dynamic fragility—should lead to a drastic rethinking of the nature of a "good" marriage. Instead the emergent Catholic "experts" on the subject seem to swallow whole the prevailing psychological cliches and attempt to impose these cliches on the Church as the standards for its own doctrine and practice.

The manner in which Catholic revisionists write about marital dissolution is reminiscent of the vague and euphemistic expressions often used to disguise the hard realities of illness and death. Especially striking is the seeming unwillingness to ask precisely why, and under what circumstances, marriages do break down. The leading clerical advocate of divorce believes that "few marriages among persons trying to lead Christian lives break up because of willfully wrong words or actions."[10] Another priest blandly asks "how can we talk about indissolubility in a world where everything dissolves; our only real constant is change."[11] A lay theologian writes about "marriages which have a built-in self-destruct mechanism that is triggered somewhere along the line by the psychic chemistry of the partners. . . ."[12]

Consider, however, another familiar contemporary scenario: a man and woman have been married for twenty years, with several children. They have, for the most part, been happy and their relationship a harmonious one. At age forty-four, however, the husband (or, perhaps increasingly now, the wife) meets someone younger and more attractive to whom he would like to be married. The new relationship brings an excitement, a freshness into his life which his wife has not induced in years. He asks for a divorce, which his wife, after her initial shock and through her continuing grief, reluctantly agrees to give him.

The simple truth is that, in modern America, many divorces take place primarily because one party (sometimes both) wishes to be married to someone else. If Christ's strictures against adultery have any relevance, it is surely in instances of this kind. Yet the Catholic apologists for divorce seem to wish to conceal from public view precisely what these often sordid moral realities really are. Formulas about "irreversible breakdown" and "self-destruct mechanism" seem designed to conceal the fact that free human choices are at the heart of divorce, not mechanical malfunctions over which the participants have no control.

The strategy of the defenders of divorce is easy enough to comprehend. It is the familiar, and understandable, one of those who wish to remove a public stigma from a particular action and seek to do so by claiming that those who engage in the action are not really responsible for what they do. Its aim is benign and compassionate.

It must be asserted, nonetheless, that such an approach to moral problems is ultimately the opposite of compassionate, just as it is the opposite of humane, if by humane is meant that which is appropriate to human beings. It ends by trivializing human nature and human behavior, by making people in effect less than fully human. For to be human means to be free. And to be free means not simply the ability to do what one wants, although there is a growing tendency to understand it in that way, but above all the ability to make real moral choices. It is this ability, which lies at the heart of being human, that apologists for divorce tend to deny, in the interests of relieving divorced persons of any moral culpability for their acts.

In this context some of the reasons offered by Catholic moralists in favor of a new order are rather startling. A noted theologian, for example, regards the tribunal procedures of the past as suited to an age when people were "less mature" than they are today.[13] A canonist also speaks of the "maturity" of today's youth, superior to that of their parents at a similar age.[14] Contrast these assertions with an account which is by no means unusual in today's world:

> "I was experiencing depression, but I didn't know why. I had a nice family, a nice husband, a nice house.

> "I was disenchanted, felt somewhat bored and didn't have self-confidence. . . ."

> To find herself, she walked out on her husband and children.[15]

To postulate "maturity" in such situations is possible only if by "maturity" is meant the willingness to place self-fulfillment above every other consideration in life. The case could easily be made that, with their low tolerance of frustration, their often unrealistically high expectations from marriage, their easily disillusioned romanticism, and their often apparent egocentrism, many married people today are in fact much less mature than in the past, that contemporary society breeds and prolongs immaturity by fostering in people the expectation that all their desires will be met.

There is operative in American society a systematic flight from responsibility on the part of people for whom all structures, institutions, traditions—everything in fact which they have not created themselves—are intrusions and impositions on their psyches, the constraints of family life most of all. Joseph Epstein, a divorced man who has written perhaps the best book on divorce, says:

> The old obligations, the given necessity of life, could be burdensome and indeed sometimes crushing, but they did provide an anchor of sorts. . . . The only necessity one need feel under today is that of enlivening one's days, making an interesting life, and discovering ever fresh possibilities for personal happiness.

He goes on to cite Kierkegaard's notion of the "excess of possibility," in which the possibility of everything makes impossible a commitment to anything in particular.[16]

But the denial of freedom which lies beneath much of the new Catholic attitude towards divorce even goes beyond the implicit denial that people are or ought to be responsible for their actions in marriage, the denial that whether or not their marriages endure has much to do with whether they choose to make them endure. It also involves a willingness to place them, and indeed the whole Church, in bondage to contemporary culture, whose prevailing norms are treated as unassailable.

Thus a priest ridicules what he calls the "finger-in-the-dike theory," by which the Church undertakes to uphold traditional values in the face of their widespread erosion in the world. Since the Church will not have a determinative voice in what marriage will be like in the late twentieth century, "I think we Roman Catholics should take our fingers out and learn how to swim in this new human era."[17] A theologian goes even farther, insisting that history mandates a change in Catholic doctrine and quoting the playwright Hendrik Ibsen, "That man is right who has allied himself most closely with the future."[18] A canon lawyer worries because non-Catholics have "passed us" in their attitudes towards divorce.[19] Attitudes of historical and cultural relativism are in fact pervasive in much of recent Catholic thinking about divorce, and everywhere the message is the same: no one has either the ability or the right to hold moral principles at variance with those which dominate the culture. Whatever might be said of this attitude, it can scarcely be said to promote genuine freedom. It inculcates in people a certain passivity, in which events are perceived merely as things which happen and in which being carried along by the movement of history is the easiest kind of response.

One priest, writing as recently as 1974, argued that the American divorce rate was no cause for alarm. Its increase was slow, he insisted, and might well be levelling off. In fact, since so many divorced people got remarried, divorce could even be seen as a tribute to people's belief in marriage. There was much cause for "hope."[20] (By this reasoning, it would seem that the more frequently people marry, the better. Permanent unions would be undesirable because they would lower the statistics on the number of marriages performed.)

In fact, as might well have been predicted even in 1974, the divorce rate in America is by no means decelerating. It reached its first high peak in the period 1945-47, then steadily declined until about 1966, since which time it has increased sharply and continues to do so. In 1955 there were about five times as many marriages performed as divorces granted, but by 1976 the ratio was barely two to one. In 1950 there were 2.6 divorces per 1000 people in the United States, but by 1976 that rate had almost doubled. Demographers from the Bureau of the Census postulate an eventual levelling off of the divorce rate but do not see it in the immediate future.[21] (The rate would be even higher were it not for the fact that many couples now choose to live together without benefit of marriage, and when they separate that fact does not appear in the statistics.)

The high divorce rate of 1945-47 is easily explicable on the basis of hasty wartime marriages followed by long separations. What, however, accounts for the enormous increases of the past decade and a half? (There were 479,000 divorces granted in America in 1965, over a million in 1976.)

There are no statistics on the reasons why people divorce (reasons offered in court are notoriously questionable in any case), so that conclusions on this point are necessarily impressionistic. One impression is strong, however—if the causes of divorce are divided into "hard" and "soft" categories, the former including specific things like violence, alcoholism, financial failure, and real desertion, the latter including general feelings of non-fulfillment or constriction, the importance of the latter seems to be rapidly growing and gaining in social respectability. A priest argues that "what we are witnessing is not a decline, but rather the positive evolution of a new kind of marriage. . . independent, dynamic and growth-oriented, and open to many expanded human relationships."[22]

It may be argued on the contrary that this "new kind of marriage" is precisely at the root of the epidemic of divorces, since it rests on assumptions and expectations which are so unrealistic as to lead to almost inevitable failure. The same priest writes:

> Our contemporaries expect more in terms of intimacy, friendship, support, and compassionship [sic!] in marriage than any generation before us. . . . Because their expectations are high, many men and women are not finding what they want. In some cases they may be unrealistic—in others they believe that they married the wrong partner.[23]

That modest word "expect" is at the root of all the trouble. The assumption of modern culture is that expectations exist in order to be met, yet classical moral wisdom (philosophical as well as religious) holds that it is often the case that human beings find happiness and truth by learning to alter their expectations.

The distinction between those who are "unrealistic" and those who believe that "they married the wrong partner" is obviously a crucial one, yet the revisionist literature on divorce does not suggest how it is to be maintained. By definition, someone who consciously thinks that his expectations are unrealistic is someone who does not suffer from that problem; it is precisely those who do not realize this who have the problem. Each person who seeks a divorce obviously believes that he had the bad fortune to pick "the wrong partner."

In times of moral revolution, very obvious and basic realities are lost sight of, usually because they have been shoved out of sight as inconvenient. The reigning popular psychology tends to skate over the fact that all human relationships require sacrifice, whatever rewards they also entail. This psychology simultaneously holds two almost contradictory ideals—self-fulfillment and "meaningful" relations with other people—without noticing that some of the most meaningful human realtionships are those in which the participants give little conscious thought to self-fulfillment.

There is now little inclination on the part of those in positions of influence to remind people of this elementary fact. Those who enter into marriage expecting an almost mystical fulfillment are not likely to find it in any case, yet the unlikelihood is enormously compounded when these same people cling also to the conviction that they must be true to themselves and surrender no iota of their individual autonomy. It bears repeating that those who have apparently achieved the new style of marriage celebrated above have not by any means thereby rendered themselves immune to marital breakdown. Impressions suggest that such people, deeply imbued with the dogmas of modern popular psychology, are among those most prone to divorce.

The ease with which divorce is accepted cannot help, in the long run, encouraging people to get divorced for relatively trivial and even frivolous reasons, and it also tends to encourage equally frivolous marriages. People enter into matrimony with the expectation that they may well fail. A first marriage may almost come to be treated by some people as a trial event for later relationships. By its ready tolerance, society conveys the unmistakable impression that it places no very heavy weight on marital permanence or fidelity.

However, of all the odd silences which characterize contemporary Catholic writing about divorce none is so odd as the assumption which seems to permeate it (an assumption never established or even discussed) that divorce is always or usually a matter of genuinely mutual desire. The picture of divorce which emerges is of a harmonious, civilized decision by two people that their marriage has "died," that they have "ceased to grow," or that they are not "fulfilled," whereupon they agree to seek a dissolution of their union for the benefit of both of them.

Reality, however impressionistically, suggests that the picture is often quite different. Marriages sometimes do dissolve by mutual consent, or a mutually growing sense of disenchantment. However, it is perhaps far more common that one party to the union first seeks to be free of the other, and the other spouse is only slowly and reluctantly persuaded to acquiesce. In many cases divorce functions as a means for the gratification of one party, with the other party victimized in the process.

The silence of Catholic writers on this question is particularly ominous in their failure to look candidly at the role which infidelity plays in contemporary marital breakdowns. Very often one person seeks a divorce not because of such lofty-sounding reasons as "failure to grow" but for the simple reason that he or she would now rather be married to someone else, and it is not cynical to suspect that lust plays a considerable role in such desires.

Literature and life are full of examples of the

man who tells his mistress, "I can't marry you because my wife is a Catholic, and she won't give me a divorce." If in art this formula is usually meant to suggest that the man simply wants the advantages of an extra-marital affair without the responsibilities of another marriage, in life it has probably often served as a means of protection for the injured wife. The revisionist writers on divorce, lawyers though some of them be, pay little attention to marriage as a network of rights and responsibilities. They prefer to see it through the tinted glasses of popular psychological dogma. Consequently in their writings there is remarkably little attention paid to the protection of rights and the likely damage done to the rights of one party in the process of divorce.

The rights in question are not primarily financial, although that certainly enters into the equation. Rather they are the rights of a person who has, in good faith, in full expectation of living up to the agreement, committed himself or herself to a lifetime of fidelity to another person. At some point this individual discovers that his or her spouse no longer wishes to be bound by the agreement. Quite possibly the spouse has already begun acting unfaithfully. For many married people this discovery can be crushing, causing a degree of pain and agony which is almost unendurable. They suddenly find themselves victimized and totally vulnerable, badly in need of whatever protection and help they can find.

Faced with a restless partner who now wants to be extricated from the marriage, the faithful partner's immediate instinct may be to exclaim, "But we committed ourselves to one another for better or for worse." This reminder is likely to be met with patient persuasion, evasive silence, or angry denial from the other side, for whom the achievement of liberation from a binding commitment is now all that matters.

Finally, however, even if the unfaithful spouse is determined to carry through with the divorce, even if in the practical order there is no likelihood of a change of heart, the objective obligation which such a person owes the faithful spouse is not thereby eliminated, nor even diminished. Should the Church, the institution which above all others reminds men of their duties to God and one another, grant its blessing and approval to an act which, at least on the part of one party, may be a gross and blatant violation of a solemn moral obligation?

In the present milieu, those spouses who do continue to regard their marital vows as binding come to seem merely priggish or psychologically rigid. Immense harm is done by Catholics, priests especially, who by words or attitudes add to burdens of faithful spouses by implying that they should be "realistic" and accept the irreversibility of marital breakdown. Many people, under such circumstances, must feel abandoned and betrayed by the Church in ways not alluded to in fashionable treatises on Catholic "insensitivity."

It is particularly odd that champions of women's rights have not placed greater emphasis on protecting the rights of faithful spouses, since it appears to be wives especially who are rendered vulnerable by the ease with which divorces are now obtained. (The explanation for their silence probably lies in the pervasive moral iconoclasm which characterizes advanced feminist thinking and the fact that the demands of Women's Liberation are primarily tailored to the desires of highly educated, upper-middle-class women.) As a woman experienced in the problems of the modern family has pointed out, middle-aged women who have not been employed for years are highly vulnerable when their husbands reject them. Defaults in alimony and child-support payments are common, and divorced women are less likely to remarry than are divorced men.[24]

When divorce becomes virtually epidemic, the question must be asked whether it does not represent an unconscious or semi-conscious rejection of marriage, whether divorces are now caused not by this or that grievance or dissatisfaction which spouses may have with one another but by a restive inability to accept the discipline of marriage itself. In other words, although in principle most people may still believe in the institution, in practice the attitudes and expectations which society instills in them may make them unfit for marriage as it has traditionally been understood.

The demand that the Catholic Church alter its "unrealistic" position on divorce would, paradoxically, have greater force if the divorce rate were relatively constant and moderate. However, as divorce becomes rampant, as more and more people get divorced, including more and more Catholics, the question must be asked if it would not be irresponsible for the Church to abandon its traditional stance. Not only would this represent a wholesale surrender to social and cultural pressures, it would also remove, at a critical juncture, one of the major moral and institutional constraints against even further erosion of the institution of marriage.

A high divorce rate, and divorces easily obtained, tend to be self-reinforcing. This is not merely in terms of conscious respectability—the fact that when divorce has a social stigma attached to it people will hesitate to get divorced—but even more in terms of unconscious expectations. When divorce seems like an unusual, possibly even strange phenomenon, many people cannot imagine themselves engaging in it. They order their lives in such a way that the possibility of divorce does not seriously enter their calculations. As a result, they are likely to regard marriage as an awesome and irrevocable step. They take quite seriously the promise of fidelity "for better or for worse." Even if unconsciously, they tend to act in their marriages on the assumption that they will remain with the same partner for many years.

Now, however, there is a widespread scepticism about marriage and its durability. In attempting to eliminate the stigma from divorce, its apologists cannot help implying that there is really nothing wrong with it, even though they may, on a formal level, call it a tragedy. As more and more people get divorced, more and more people are encouraged to get divorced, for several reasons: because divorce now seems normal, because it often seems a more attractive solution to marital frustration than self-sacrifice or lowered expectations of happiness, and because the expectation grows that a high proportion of marriages will fail and many people unconsciously expect their own marriages to be among that number.

It is not unfair to say that divorce is on its way to becoming almost an ideal in American society.

For although it continues to be acknowledged as tragic and painful, it is also increasingly thought of as an experience which most people are likely to have at some time in their lives. Since society worships "experience" as the chief source of knowledge and the chief means by which personal maturity is attained, it may well be the case before long that the burden of proof, as it were, will shift from those who are divorced to those who are not.

Those who are divorced will be thought of as people who have continued to grow, who have remained "open to new experiences." The likelihood of anyone's choosing the "right" spouse on the first try will be thought rather small. Furthermore, the "right" spouse at age twenty-five will be considered a different person from the "right" spouse at age forty. People have a tendency to develop in different directions, so that a permanent union must become in time an artificial and strained yoking. Despite its pain, divorce will be thought of as a strengthening experience, and those who get divorced will be praised for their courage and honesty. Meanwhile there will be a spirit of scepticism about the permanently married—does their union truly represent love and commitment, or merely timidity, stodginess, the gradual closing of all the avenues of personal growth? In certain social contexts, divorce will become not merely a right but virtually an obligation.

It is startling, for example, to hear a canon lawyer apparently give the "right" to a second marriage precedence over the right to marry a first time, on the grounds that the experience of divorce has created a "need" which must be filled. Divorce itself is regarded not only as a possibility but frequently as a "necessity," and the Church is urged to encourage divorce in some instances.[25] Another priest rejoices that divorced Catholics are "much farther ahead than the clergy and the bishops" and appears to cast them in the role of moral leaders of the future Church.[26]

The same avant-garde priest has been unusually frank in admitting that "the male-dominated, child-centered, ethnically-defined marriage of the past several hundred years is coming apart. . . ."[27] Allowing for certain prejudicial terms (official male domination has often been something quite different in practice), this is precisely what most people, certainly most Catholics, have experienced as marriage and family life. They are thus being given fair warning that, despite what is sometimes asserted, Catholic acceptance of divorce has direct links to the undermining of traditional family life.

Joseph Epstien has observed the contemporary marital scene:

> Patriarchy is dead, replaced not by matriarchy, the rule of women, but by a variety of psychic Marxism in marriage, which holds that to each is accorded his own emotional needs—provided, of course, that these needs do not conflict with the emotional needs of the marriage partner. If the emotional needs do conflict—which they cannot help but do, in many cases frequently and irreconcilably—well, that is what divorce courts are for.
>
> The dissolution of the family, evidenced in the loss of feeling between husbands and wives and in the absence of regard between parents and children, represents the culminating point of the dissolution of all sense of community. The family and the community, after all, long shared a deep bond of reciprocity: a community was built on the strength of the families within it. . . .
>
> What the loss of a sense of community involves . . . is the loss of the ability to imagine that one's actions have any consequence outside one's own life. . . . the accompanying inability to imagine anything more important than one's own happiness.[28]

Divorce, like other actions related to human sexual behavior, is coming to have a privileged status among moral acts, in the sense that (like such things as homosexuality and, in the minds of many, abortion) society is asked to treat those who engage in it as persons of such unquestionable personal sincereity and deep moral sensitivity as to be beyond even questioning, to say nothing of criticism or condemnation. The rightness of divorce is assumed in virtually every case, and those who would subject it to even ordinary kinds of moral scrutiny are often angrily rebuffed as rigid and fanatical. It is quite startling, for example, to learn that a prominent canon lawyer believes that, in any application for an annulment of marriage, the burden of proof should be placed on those who defend the bond, not on those who challenge it.[29]

The result of this line of reasoning is to refuse in effect to defend the legitimacy of marital vows at all. The stability of marriage and the sacredness of its vows are not deemed important enough to warrant such a defense, and in fact the tribunals are even denied a moral right to mount one. The absurd implication of such reasoning, whether or not intended, is that all existing marriages are to be presumed invalid unless proof can be offered to the contrary. So long as no one raises the issue, the Church would presumably be content to treat most marriages as though they were valid. However, as soon as the participants in a marriage allege that it is invalid, the Church would immediately accept their word. The contempt for the very idea of marital permanency which is here implied is not redeemed by the doubtlessly benign intentions which lie behind this eagerness to dissolve marriages with as little resistance as possible, this apparent refusal even to raise the issue of validity.

Catholic revisionists are nowhere more naive than in their failure to recognize that divorce is one of the weapons in the arsenal from which the primacy of the family as a social institution is now under attack. And yet some of them are aware of it, however dimly. The same canonist who wishes to place the burden of proof on those who would defend the validity of marriage also postulates a growing "personalism" and "maturity" about sex among young people, a maturity which seems to leave open the real possibility of "premarital and postmarital affection."[30] An influential psychologist and former priest finds "wisdom" in young people living together without benefit of marriage, for which they are "not yet in sufficient possession of themselves."[31] A European theologian argues, in the context of a plea for more permissive attitudes towards divorce, for a radical rethinking of Christian sexual ethics and finds pre-marital sex also quite permissible.[32]

What is simultaneously the most bizarre and, in another sense, the most natural moral linkage which has occurred is between divorce and polygamy, however far-fetched the connection may at first seem. A collective international cry for the Church to take a more "realistic" and "compassionate" view of divorce includes, for example, a strong plea for the moral permissibility of polygamy, at least in those cultures where it is commonly practiced.[33] In America one of the first books by a Catholic theologian justifying divorce includes arguments not only for the legitimacy of pre-marital and extra-marital sex (couples living together are to be regarded as already married) but also for euthanasia, "triangular relationships," sexual therapy in non-marital encounters, extra-marital affairs, and polygamy. In fact the author urges that the Catholic Church not only permit polygamy but actively promote it and agitate for the repeal of civil laws prohibiting it. (He sees it as having practical advantages, especially for groups of older people, in which women commonly outnumber men.) Sperm banks, by which the begetting of children need no longer be the exclusive or even primary responsibility of the "father" of the family, are also favored.[34]

Although such connections may seem arbitrary, they have a certain logic to them. For if divorce is the denial of the ultimately binding character of monogamous marriage, and if the bond can be dissolved for the sake of such things as "growth" and "personal fulfillment," then no one can say with any certitude that divorce alone will suffice. Many people may find (many already are finding) that a succession of marriages to different partners does not really relieve the problem, because the problem is precisely the requirement of committing oneself to a single partner, on however temporary a basis. The arguments used to discredit particular marriages can often be used to discredit marriage in general. Those who find marriage to a particular individual "intolerable" and who ask "understanding" and "compassion" from the Church (as well as that the Church become more "realistic" and more contemporary in its attitudes) can, with equal fervor and logic, ask the Church to be "trusting" and "non-judgmental" towards any number of sexual relationships which involve the deliberate rejection of the monogamous family.

In the midst of an almost global crisis, what should be the Church's response to divorce? The weakest suggested response is yet another invocation of that blessed liberal panacea—education. Pre-marital counseling and the inculcating of a realistic attitude towards marriage are commonly advocated as the best contributions the Church could make to marital stability and fidelity.

No one can be opposed to education. However, it needs to be recognized that the generation presently getting divorced in unprecedented numbers is the best-educated generation in the history of the world, both in general and with regard to sex and marriage. Even divorcees from the poorer classes are relatively more educated than were their often totally illiterate laborer or peasant forebears, and apart from formal schooling they have much greater access to the larger world, through the mass media.

Those Americans now in their twenties, whose marriages are unravelling at so rapid a pace, are precisely the generation which has enjoyed the maximum benefits of education and continue to enjoy the benefits of trained professionals available to offer help for all manner of marital problems—psychological, sexual, or financial.

To point out this fact is not to say that such education is a cause of marital breakdown, nor to argue that it should be abolished. It is, however, to point out that the prevailing liberal faith in education, in this as in so many other areas, often ends by being deeply disappointed. (Contrary to what sex educators have been predicting for many years, the number of illegitimate pregnancies does not decrease as formal sex education increases, but rather the reverse.)

Finally, the reason why "education" consistently proves so disappointing is that, as every teacher knows, moral attitudes are notoriously difficult to influence through formal instruction.

Yet the roots of marriage are primarily moral ones, and whether marriages are strong or fragile finally rests on the moral values of the spouses, which it is doubtful any amount of formal education will influence deeply, especially at times when stresses have already entered the marriage.

A stronger suggestion for the Catholic role in countering marital breakdown is that the Church exists to uphold the "ideal" of marital permanency, of life-long fidelity, that it uses moral suasion and example but does not invoke authority nor sanction.[35]

However, as G. K. Chesterton wrote many years ago, "I take it, however, that the advocates of divorce do not mean that marriage is to remain ideal only in the sense of being almost impossible. They do not mean that a faithful husband is only to be admired as a fanatic."[36] Written half in jest at a time when the divorce rate was, by present-day standards, extremely low, these words have become sharply prophetic.

Catholic apologists for divorce have first failed to grasp to what extent marriage and lifelong fidelity are no longer, for many people, even an ideal, how many people refuse to commit themselves to a marital relationship or, if they do, revise their vows to exclude all reference to permanency. Furthermore, this reduced respect even for the ideal of marriage is directly related to the phenomenon of divorce in typically circular fashion, as both cause and effect.

Christian ideals are meant to be lived up to, and when more and more people appear to be falling short of doing so, there is surely a necessity for concern. When people get into the habit of thinking of any difficult moral demand as "merely" an ideal, they also get into the habit of thinking of it as unattainable. Furthermore, as contemporary culture demonstrates abundantly, an ideal which comes to be thought of as unattainable soon ceases to be even an ideal and is regarded as something which is, at best, appropriate for a few unusual people and quite possibly, as Chesterton joked, a manifestation of fanaticism.

Most Protestant churches have settled for an attitude towards marriage which stresses the "ideal" of permanency while making concessions to weak humanity. However the extent of those concessions has broadened measurably. Many churches provide their members with opportunities for marital counseling. Few, apparently, attempt to use strong moral suasion to persuade married couples not to divorce, nor is the ideal of permanency held up as an awesome thing which the individual falls short of only with trepidation. The "therapeutic" attitude described by Philip Rieff requires that moral burdens not be laid on fragile consciences. Every effort must be made by clergy and counsellors to be "supportive," "non-judgmental," and "compassionate."

One of the greatest services the Church can offer humanity in the present crisis is precisely to witness to the belief that the permanency of marriage is an ideal which is attainable, and in practice this means sometimes issuing reminders—stern reminders, if necessary—to particular individuals that they are acting irresponsibly and undermining that ideal in their lives. Often this will mean refusing to bless a second marriage.

Numerous attempts have been made to offer purely verbal solutions to the problem, formulas which appear simultaneously to uphold the traditional doctrine while allowing for modern accommodations. One theologian, for example, argues, bewilderingly, that the "Gospel ideal" of indissolubility is somehow "enhanced" if the Church sanctions divorce.[37] Another theologian holds that the sanctioning of second marriages would not in any way mark a change in traditional doctrine,[38] while a canon lawyer appears satisfied with the slogan, "it is the bond, not the bondage, that is important."[39]

Yet for the Catholic Church to sanction marriage after divorce, no matter how carefully the practice were hedged about with verbal qualifications and explanations, would be popularly (and rightly) understood as a change of doctrine. Such practice would, inevitably, be taken as an admission of past error and a belated and somewhat embarrassed accommodation to modern realities.

A "pastoral" solution has been proposed—that the Church continue to forbid divorce and refuse to bless second marriages, while subsequently admitting divorced and remarried persons to the sacraments. Whether this is a tenable solution to a practical dilemma is debatable. No less a personage than the principal clerical advocate of legitimized divorce has argued that such a policy "would, in effect, both uphold the law and reward the law-breaker. It would breed further contempt for church law."[40]

As a theologian has pointed out, if the first marriages of the remarried partners are still valid, then the symbolism of this "reconciliation" to the Church would be false. There would occur a "clash of symbols."[41] The accuracy of this assertion is, unwittingly, confirmed by a priest who favors the policy of readmitting divorced persons to the sacraments. He suggests that, under such a system, "the past is forgotten."[42] Yet how can the past be forgotten if the first marriage is still valid?

Divorced people now frequently ask, and have a right to ask, why divorce should be treated differently from many other sins. Why does a Church which gives its sacraments to gangsters, racists, and corrupt politicians refuse them to divorced people? Is divorce the worst of all possible sins?

The major reason why divorce is treated differently from other sins is twofold—the fact that it is public and formal and the fact that while it persists there can be no real possibility of repentance.

Priests who may have strong suspicions to the contrary are nonetheless obligated to give the individual the benefit of the doubt, unless incontrovertible proof is offered. Occasionally the Church does pronounce excommunication against those who have openly and officially aligned themselves with racist organizations or other groups whose doctrines clearly contradict Christian teaching.

Divorce, however, is of its nature a public act, an act involving a formal and legal relationship. It is something which cannot, therefore, be ignored (although there are doubtlessly cases of divorced and remarried people who conceal this fact from their priests). It differs in this sense from adultery, where in the absence of undeniable proof a priest would again be obligated to give an individual the benefit of the doubt.

Secondly, every sin requires at least the claim of repentance. And, insofar as it is possible, the penitent must attempt to undo the evil effects of the sin. In the case of divorce the sin is precisely the dissolution of a marital bond, the repudiation of a commitment solemnly made in the sight of God. Thus the claim of repentance would necessarily involve some attempt on the part of the divorced person once again to honor that commitment.

If the divorced person's first spouse is dead, there is no real problem, since in Catholic practice the new marriage can be blessed and regularized in the eyes of the Church (assuming the second spouse is not also divorced). If the first spouse has long disappeared, some presumption might be made in favor of the second marriage. But if (as is perhaps usually the case) the first spouse is now married to someone else, the fact must be recognized that according to a Catholic understanding of the marriage vows, such a second marriage does not release the divorced partner from his or her original commitment, although some consideration might be given in cases where one of the partners sincerely repents the original divorce but the other partner refuses any reconcilation.

Realistically, however, it may be asked how

many divorced people actually do repent, in the sense of being sincerely sorry for having divorced and wishing to undo its effects as much as they are able. Much more common seems to be the case of divorced persons who are not prepared to admit that they have done anything wrong, who perceive no sin, and who may even be angry at the Church for suggesting that sin is involved. For such people the idea of "repentance" has no meaning. They refuse to accept the moral implications of what they have done, and all talk of repentance is merely a verbal formula to gloss over profound theological difficulties. The very fact that they seek ecclesiastical recognition of their second (or third) marriages is based, usually, on their belief that these later unions are somehow better than the first one.

Many married Catholics may be far more sinful in the sight of God than many of the divorced. But in no way does this dictate that the Church should recognize a practice which it knows to be wrong.

Yet another proposed solution to the problem of divorce among Catholics is the "good conscience" clause, according to which divorced Catholics whose consciences assure them of the invalidity of their first marriage and the consequent validity of the second would approach the sacraments on that basis.

In the post-conciliar Church, "conscience" has become a word to conjure with, so that anyone invoking such a solution automatically gains a respectful hearing, and no one can afford to be thought to be against conscience. Nonetheless, it is worth noting certain inadequacies in this concept.

Traditionally conscience has been commonly used in a negative sense—it is that moral faculty which calls the individual to an awareness of duty. Conscience has been most acute when it instructs people in the obligation to perform certain acts which they would perhaps prefer not to perform (as for example, when referring to a "conscientious person," or "my conscience bothers me.")

Now the word is more commonly used to mean that moral faculty which assures people that what they wish to do is not wrong. It is a faculty which, rather than calling one to duty and difficult decisions, gives assurance of moral rectitude and of the fact that the desired course of action is the correct one. Such an understanding of conscience is not altogether incorrect, since conscience is a discriminatory faculty which ought to exclude excessive scrupulosity as well as excessive permissiveness. However, the word is now commonly used primarily in the former sense, as a faculty which in effect gives the individual assurance of moral rightness in situations where there might be doubt about his conduct.

For the individual to say, "My conscience is clear on this question," is hardly to bring an end to the matter. The question of the correctness of that judgment still remains open. Bluntly put, how far can conscience be trusted? Is not human nature such that conscience easily becomes lax, easily tells the individual simply what he or she wants to believe? In law there is a wise principle that no man should be judge in his own case. Applied to marriage and divorce, it seems obvious that the pressure for self-justification will often be extremely strong among Catholics who know they have done something which traditional Catholic teaching deems wrong. The contention that such people can, with balance and honesty, judge whether or not their own actions are morally right is to place much too heavy a load on the individual conscience.

Above all the question must be blunty faced: Should the Church simply accept the word of those who say that in good conscience their first marriages were never valid? Is human testimony, especially in so sensitive and emotional an area of life, really so trustworthy as to require no objective corroboration?

It might be suggested that divorced Catholics

have been badly served by their theological and legal champions. The arguments advanced in favor of divorce and remarriage are such that for the Church to accept them would be tantamount to undermining its entire matrimonial discipline and the sacredness of its sacraments. The needs of divorced Catholics have been ill-served by tying those needs to currently fashionable moral attitudes which are ultimately destructive of all moral responsibility. Despite the failings of their champions, divorced Catholics do suffer, and their needs should not be dismissed merely on the basis of the dubious ways in which their claims have been presented.

They are, unquestionably, entitled to genuine pastoral solicitude from the Church, something which in the past they have not always received. If divorced people are treated as moral outcasts, or if priests show that they have no time for the divorced, a serious dereliction of responsibility occurs.

Pastoral solicitude does not, however, necessarily involve granting moral approval to divorce, or relieving the consciences of the divorced from any idea of their having done wrong. True pastoral concern always involves setting consciences right, and it might sometimes involve a measure of severity, since a lax conscience is destructive to the person who possesses it, and correcting such laxity is an act of love.

However, pastoral concern does mean the willingness of priests and others in pastoral situations to listen to the troubles and questions of those caught in the painful situation of divorce. It means showing respect and sympathy for such people, a willingness to explore with them the peculiar problems of their situation and how these might be resolved, and attempting to integrate them into the life of the Church as far as possible. While much of Catholic parish life is inevitably family-oriented, this does not mean that divorced people need to be made to feel excluded or unwelcome. Special apostolates to the divorced, retreats designed especially for them, and organizations for their help are belated but important innovations.

There undoubtedly exist marriages which are indeed intolerable, at least for one of the parties, and where separation and divorce may be, humanly speaking, the only possible solution. Unions which are truly intolerable (as distinct from being merely uncomfortable) are probably rather rare, but they do exist—cases, for example, where one partner is an unreformed alcoholic, or is prone to violence, or apparently has no real commitment to marital fidelity and no real sense of responsibility.

The idea that what seems humanly right is

always what is right in the sight of God has gained rapid ground in recent years, to the point where many Catholics sincerely cannot conceive any other possibility. Yet Christianity has always taught that God's ways are often not man's ways, and in situations where the only human solution to a bad marriage seems to be divorce it is perhaps the Church's duty to recognize that this may be a practical necessity while at the same time refusing to give it religious and moral sanction.

In the present climate of opinion little attention is paid to another pastoral work which the Church is in a unique position to perform, and that is to aid divorced people who accept the binding nature of their first marriage and who therefore resolve to remain unmarried during the lifetime of their first spouse.

So pervasive are certain psychological dogmas that the immediate response to such a suggestion is likely to be one of scepticism and even derision. Yet countless numbers of Catholics have, because of the seriousness with which they take their marital vows and the law of God, chosen precisely such a life. Their voices need to be heard in the present discussion, their sometimes very impressive moral witness needs to be taken account of. In its true sense, pastoral care involves showing people the full range of spiritual possibilities open to them. The possibility that divorced people may live meaningful celibate lives, that such a possibility may in fact involve unique opportunities for spiritual growth, is one which the Church ought not lightly to dismiss, however unfashionable it may be.

ANNULMENT

Annulment is quite different from divorce, in that it is a declaration by the Church that a real marriage never existed. It has, for many centuries, been the way in which Catholics involved in intolerable marriages have sought to be released from them.

Since annulment is not divorce, it will not be discussed in detail here. Several points seem worth making, however. Since the Second Vatican Council there have been two developments of importance with regard to annulments—a tremendous increase in the number granted (at least in the United States) and the extension of the grounds for annulment to include the "psychological norms."

The increase in numbers is not in itself necessary cause for concern, since it appears that prior to the Council many diocesan tribunals were unnecessarily rigid in granting annulments and that a prudent but more flexible policy would necessarily result in an increase. In principle the "psychological norms" also seem proper and desirable. They involve the recognition that there are sometimes aspects of personality which make it difficult or even impossible for certain people really to commit themselves to marriage, and that their marriages are of a consequence fatally flawed from the beginning.

However, there are also grounds for disquiet in the way in which some diocesan tribunals now administer annulments. In Brooklyn, for example, the tribunal granted 628 annulments in 1977 and did not refuse a single one. A very liberal canon lawyer has charged that some tribunals are in effect granting divorces while calling them annulments. Some tribunals seem indisposed to discover any valid marriages at all, and it can only be assumed that the very loose criteria of invalidity which they apply could have the effect of invalidating almost any marraige. The criterion of "psychological incapacity"—the declaration that a certain person was incapable of entering into matrimony at the time when he or she did so—also, as the same canonist points out, has the effect of trivializing human freedom and demeaning human dignity. Often those whose first marriages have been declared invalid because of "incapacity" are immediately granted permission to enter into a second marriage, the incapacity having apparently disappeared.[43]

Perhaps the greatest failing of those who advocate a new Catholic approach to divorce is their failure to discuss it in the context of marriage, without which context they are virtually doomed to adopt a wholly secular perspective.

The Second Vatican Council, in this as in so many other matters far from the innovative gathering it is often made out to be, referred to the "plague of divorce," which it linked with "so-called free love." It reminded Catholics that God is the author of marriage, not human beings.[44]

For Christians the central and dominating idea of marriage must be the union of man and woman as Christ loves His Church (Ephesians 5:25). Such a daring and sublime concept forever raises human marriage above the purely utilitarian and pragmatic and gives it a profound mystical significance. The Second Vatican Council said that "authentic married love is caught up into divine love and is directed and enriched by the redemptive power of Christ and the salvific action of the Church." Marriage thus becomes for the married their principal means of sanctity.[45]

In modern times, as always, it is precisely the unpredictability of their commitments which troubles people about marriage, but it is also characteristic of modern times that more and more people believe that a commitment which issues in something they had not anticipated is a commitment which is no longer binding. Yet if vows do not apply above all to situations of this kind, then they scarcely apply at all, since those who are completely content with the outcome of their commitments will obviously not be inclined to renege on them. The Second Vatican Council said that "outstanding courage is required for the constant fulfillment of the duties of this Christian calling."[46]

Marriage, it has been suggested, is not a contract as the world understands a contract, that is, a mutual agreement entered into for mutual benefit, which may be dissolved at some future time by another mutual agreement. Rather it has been described as a covenant precisely like the covenant between God and His people. It is permanent and irrevocable and engages the participants' whole being.[47]

Ultimately not even the innocent party can be granted a right to a genuine divorce because marriage is not merely a bilateral agreement; it involves God as well, and God's willingness to permit the abrogation of the covenant cannot be so easily assumed. Divorce is in its very essence a secular thing, an action which denies the presence of God in the marriage, and the acceptability of divorce among many Catholics is a major manifestation of their willingness to understand marriage in an essentially secular way. True vows are made in the presence of God, witnessed by the Church, and they cannot be repudiated simply on the wishes of those who make them. Second marriages tend to be notoriously unstable, much more so than first marriages. A 1978 estimate, by a priest working with divorced Catholics, was that over forty percent of second marriages end in divorce.[48] By refusing to give its blessing to second marriages the Church may therefore be looking quite realistically at human society.

In the end, a valid understanding of Christian marriage must understand it ontologically, as a really existing thing whose existence is not negated by the subjective state of the spouses. As a theologian has said, the marriage bond is sacramental, not merely existential. The spouses continue to belong to each other even if they stray.[49]

The age does not find it easy to think in such categories, and many will immediately dismiss them as meaningless. Yet finally they will prove to be more profound, more humane, truer, and more genuinely compassionate than habits of mind which do not take human relationships with nearly such seriousness and do not accord to them nearly such exalted possibilities. As the Second Vatican Council concluded its discourse on marriage:

> Let married people themselves, who are created in the image of the living God and constituted in an authentic personal dignity, be united together in equal affection, agreement of mind, and mutual holiness. Thus, in the footsteps of Christ, the principle of life, they will bear witness by their faithful love in the joys and sacrifices of their calling, to that mystery of love which the Lord revealed to the world by his death and resurrection.[50]

PART TWO NOTES

[1] For a sampling of discussion of the New Testament treatment of marriage see: Dominic Crossan, O.S.M., "Divorce and Remarriage in the New Testament," *The Bond of Marriage,* ed. William W. Bassett (Notre Dame, Ind., 1968), pp. 1-40; George W. Macrae, S.J., "New Testament Perspectives on Marriage and Divorce," *Divorce and Remarriage in the Catholic Church,* ed. Lawrence G. Wrenn (New York, 1973), pp. 1-15; Paul Hoffmann, "Jesus' Saying about Divorce and Its Interpretation in the New Testament Tradition," *The Future of Marriage as Institution,* ed. Franz Böckle (*Concilium,* LV [1970], pp. 51-66; Joseph A. Fitzmyer, S.J., "The Matthean Divorce Texts and Some New Palestinian Evidence," *Theological Studies,* June 1976, pp. 197-226.

[2] Macrae, "New Testament Perspectives," pp. 11-12.

[3] Hoffmann, "Jesus' Saying," p. 53.

[4] Stephen J. Kelleher, *Divorce and Remarriage for Catholics?* (Garden City, N.Y., 1973), p. 103. Msgr. Kelleher is the former presiding judge of the New York archdiocesan tribunal.

[5] Dennis J. Doherty, *Divorce and Remarriage: Resolving a Catholic Dilemma* (St. Meinrad, Ind., 1974), p. 123.

[6] Philip Rieff, *The Triumph of the Therapeutic* (New York, 1964). This book is a profound analysis of the modern cultural crisis.

[7] Wrenn, *Divorce and Remarriage,* p. 146.

[8] Kelleher, *Divorce and Remarriage,* pp. 8, 84-85.

[9] John W. Higgins in *The Bond of Marriage* (ed. Bassett), p. 212.

[10] Kelleher, *Divorce and Remarriage,* p. 49.

[11] James J. Young, C.S.P., "Misimpressions about Marriage," *Commonweal,* November 22, 1974, p. 187.

[12] Doherty, *Divorce and Remarriage,* p. 75.

[13] Bernard Häring, C.Ss.R., in *Divorce and Remarriage* (ed. Wrenn) p. 22.

[14] Kelleher, *Divorce and Remarriage,* p. 96.

[15] Bob Tamarkin, "Giving Up Family Life for New Life," *St. Louis Post-Dispatch,* August 14, 1977, p. 60.

[16] *Divorced in America: Marriage in an Age of Possibility* (New York, 1974), p. 96.

[17] Young, "Misimpressions," pp. 187-88.

[18] Doherty, *Divorce and Remarriage,* p. 54.

[19] Kelleher, *Divorce and Remarriage,* p. 104.

[20] Young, "Misimpressions," p. 188, and "Stabilizing Marriage by Permitting Divorce," *National Catholic Reporter,* February 1, 1974, p. 12.

[21] *Statistical Abstracts of the United States, 1977* (Washington, 1978), pp. 55, 74. See also Albert J. Norton and Paul C. Glick, "Marital Instability: Past, Present, and Future," *Journal of Social Issues,* XXXII, 1 (1976), pp. 6-18.

[22] Young, "Stabilizing Marriage," p. 9.

[23] Young, "Misimpressions," p. 188.

[24] Virginia A. Heffernan, "Divorce and Remarriage in the Contemporary United States," *Communio,* Fall 1974, pp. 287-89. Mrs. Heffernan is director of the family life office of the National Council of Catholic Women.

[25] Kelleher, *Divorce and Remarriage,* pp. 7-8, 79.

[26] Young, "Misimpressions," p. 190.

[27] Young, "Stabilizing Marriage," p. 9.

[28] *Divorced in America, pp. 88, 94-95.*

[29] Kelleher, *Divorce and Remarriage,* pp. 21-25.

[30] *Ibid.,* p. 96.

[31] Eugene C. Kennedy, in *Divorce and Remarriage* (ed. Wrenn), p. 127.

[32] C. Jaime Snoek in *The Future of Marriage* (ed. Böckle), pp. 111, 120.

[33] Eugene Hillman, C.S.Sp., in *ibid.,* pp. 25-38.

[34] Doherty, *Divorce and Remarriage,* pp. 34, 139, 130, 141, 149.

[35] See for example Macrae in *Divorce and Remarriage* (ed. Wrenn), p. 12; Crossan in *The Bond of Marriage* (ed. Bassett),

pp. 31-33; and Charles Curran, "Two Signs of the Times," *National Catholic Reporter,* October 18, 1974, p. 14.

[36] *The Superstition of Divorce* (New York, 1920), p. 134.

[37] Doherty, *Divorce and Remarriage,* p. 80.

[38] Häring in *The Future of Marriage* (ed. Böckle), p. 129.

[39] Bassett, *Bond of Marriage,* p. 147.

[40] Kelleher in *America,* March 15, 1975, p. 182.

[41] Paul F. Palmer. S.J., in *ibid.,* January 11, 1975, p. 11.

[42] Young in *ibid.,* p. 12.

[43] See Kelleher, *Divorce and Remarriage,* p. 118. Philip Nobile, "Brooklyn: Reno of the Catholic Church," *New York,* June 12, 1978, p. 47; Kelleher, "Catholic Annulments: a Dehumanizing Process," *Commonweal,* June 10, 1977, p. 366.

[44] *Documents of Vatican II,* Austin P. Flannery, ed. (Grand Rapids, Mich., 1975), pp. 949-50. The Council treated marriage primarily in its decree *Gaudium et Spes* ("On the Church in the Modern World").

[45] *Ibid., p. 951.*

[46] *Ibid.,* p. 952.

[47] Palmer, "Christian Marriage: Convenant or Contract?" *Theological Studies,* XXXIII (1972), pp. 635-39, and "Needed: a Theology of Marriage," *Communio,* Fall 1974, pp. 243-60.

[48] James Young, quoted in the *St. Louis Review,* July 14, 1978, p. 4.

[49] Palmer, "When a Marriage Dies," *America,* February 22, 1975, p. 127.

[50] *Documents of Vatican II,* p. 957.